Lighter than Air

An illustrated history of the development of hot-air balloons and airships

Lighter than Air

An illustrated history of the development
of hot-air balloons and airships

David Owen

APPLE

A QUINTET BOOK

Published by The Apple Press
6 Blundell Street
London N7 9BH

ISBN 1-84092-150-1

This book was designed and produced by
Quintet Publishing Limited
6 Blundell Street
London N7 9BH

Creative Director: Richard Dewing
Art Director: Simon Daley
Designer: James Lawrence
Project Editor: Debbie Foy

Typeset in Great Britain by
Central Southern Typesetters, Eastbourne
Manufactured in China by Regent Publishing Services Ltd.
Printed in Singapore by Star Standard Industries (PTE) Ltd.

Contents

Introduction

To anyone fascinated by aviation in all its forms, lighter-than-air flight has a special appeal. It opens a window on another kind of flying, following a different route from the ideas which created today's airliners, military jets, and helicopters. Mainstream flying has developed an almost unbelievably sophisticated technology. Passengers can cross the Atlantic faster than a rifle bullet on the very threshold of space, in an atmosphere so thin and cold that survival outside the pressurized cabin would call for a space-suit. The latest generation of super-agile fighters would be unmanageable death-traps, were it not for the computer software to link the pilot's commands to the aircraft's control surfaces.

Against this complex and challenging background, the elegant and graceful simplicities of lighter-than-air flight go far beyond the day the Wright Brothers ushered in the dawn of heavier-than-air flying. The story begins more than 200 years ago, when the very act of flying was a gift, to be seized by the brave and the inventive, who longed for the freedom to soar with the birds, far above the earth in the boundless space of the still unexploited third dimension.

It's an inspiring story for many different reasons. Present-day airplanes are immensely strong constructions of specialized materials, stainless steel, duralumin, and carbon-fiber composites. The first lighter-than-air flights took place in frighteningly fragile structures of wood, wire, silk, and paper, harnessing the energy of furnaces burning noxious mixtures of wool, straw, and rotten meat. Theories as to why flight was possible were confusing and often entirely wrong. But these impossibly brave pioneers persevered, attempting greater and greater challenges on their self-imposed progress to safer and more predictable flying.

It is also a story of determination. When it was clear that balloon flight was essentially limited to going wherever the breeze chose to take them, the early aeronauts dreamed of the dirigible, a steerable airship which could determine its own course under its own power. They experimented with steam and clockwork, electricity and the internal combustion engine. The airships they built grew larger and more powerful, until a new means of luxury travel and a formidable new weapon grew from their innocent attempts to fly where they wanted to go, rather than passively riding the wind.

It also has a measure of tragedy. The deaths of so many of the pioneers when their frail technology was overwhelmed by the elements were later to be echoed by the casualties when airships went to war. Peacetime disasters provided a constant counterpoint to each hopeful new advance. Airships were torn apart in thunderstorms or forced down into the sea. Even the huge and lavishly-equipped Zeppelins, which carried wealthy passengers around the world, were to prove fatally vulnerable to the very gases which gave them the power of flight. The loss of the *Hindenburg* over Lakehurst, New Jersey, when it burst into flames at the very end of a flight from Europe signaled the end of three decades of hopeful experiment and proud endeavor. More than 50 years ago, it seemed that lighter-than-air flight was an activity on its way to banishment within the pages of aviation's history books.

Yet it's also a story with immeasurable hope for the future. In the last half-century, both branches of lighter-than-air flight have seen an unexpected and dramatic renaissance. The huge revival of ballooning, which arose from a research project to develop an escape and rescue mechanism for downed military pilots, reached right back to the 1780s and the hot-air balloon which first hoisted men and women into the sky. Using synthetic materials instead of silk, and propane burners instead of wool, straw, and meat, a new worldwide industry developed, making balloons of every shape and size, and opening up a world of airborne leisure to millions of enthusiasts.

Airships too have enjoyed a welcome return to popularity. For almost three decades after the *Hindenburg* disaster, the US Navy used small, non-rigid airships filled with inherently safe helium gas to patrol the sealanes and watch for hostile submarines. The design of these simple and dependable little dirigibles has been developed into a new generation of advertising and observation craft, capable of staying aloft over a designated location with a fraction of the noise and expense of a helicopter.

Finally, it's a story worth telling. In the new century, there is every chance that bigger and more ambitious airships will soon be lifting off into the skies, to carry passengers with space and luxury no airliner can hope to match. Projects are in hand for airships as communications relay stations, or to hoist large and awkward loads to and from destinations impossibly far from the nearest airstrip. As well as a glorious past, lighter-than-air flight has a possibly limitless future.

David Owen

1. Race for the Skies

ABOVE: *The first balloon flight – the ascent of the Montgolfier unmanned hot-air balloon from Annonay*

ABOVE RIGHT: *Joseph Montgolfier – the man who started it all*

Many people believe the Air Age began in December 1903, when the Wright brothers' *Flyer* staggered into the air over the sand dunes of Kitty Hawk in North Carolina. Not so: it was really born 120 years before, and on the other side of the world.

It was a long and difficult birth, with several possible dates. One contender is Thursday, 5 June 1783, when an amazing event took place in the main square of Annonay, a small country town in southern France.

Held down by eight strong men, a huge sphere of cloth lined with paper struggled for its freedom over a large open fire. At a signal from a prosperous local paper merchant named Joseph Montgolfier, the huge framework—110 feet in circumference—rose steadily into the air.

It was the first public flight of the world's first hot-air balloon. With no passengers to weigh it down, it soared effortlessly

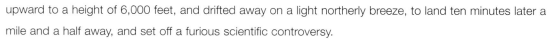

upward to a height of 6,000 feet, and drifted away on a light northerly breeze, to land ten minutes later a mile and a half away, and set off a furious scientific controversy.

Yet, to the scholars of the French Academy of Sciences, this flight was impossible. A balloon could ascend only if it was filled with a gas lighter than the air it displaced. The only known gas of this type was hydrogen, and heating an open envelope containing hydrogen over a fire was impossible. Either the hydrogen would leak away in seconds, or the balloon would explode (see box on page 11).

The Academy decided to mount its own experiment, to make a hydrogen balloon fly. In the meantime, it invited the Montgolfiers to fly their balloon in Paris, before the Academy and the King himself, to give them a closer look at this spectacle.

An Academy member, a 27-year-old physicist named Jacques Alexandre César Charles, set to work making a hydrogen balloon. He used the finest silk, coated with rubber solution, for a gas-tight envelope. To meet the costs, tickets were sold, each allowing three people to watch the ascent from a special walled enclosure within the Place des Victoires in Paris.

Although the finished envelope would be much smaller than the Montgolfier balloon, just 12 feet across, generating enough gas would be difficult. They decided to pour sulfuric acid over 1,000 pounds of iron filings, and tried mixing the chemicals in lead-lined compartments, and then in casks, but they met a whole series of problems which frustrated their attempts.

The chemical reaction made the envelope too hot, so they had to cool it with buckets of water. This caused water vapor in the gas to condense, so they had to remove it. The gas was also highly acidic, and burned holes in the fabric. Finally, it took four days to inflate the balloon to the point where they could let it climb to 100 feet, held down by ropes. The sight was too much for the crowds, who climbed the wall into the enclosure where the team were still struggling with the balloon.

To prevent damage to the balloon, they decided to move the flight to the Champ de Mars, now the site of the Eiffel Tower. The inflated balloon was lashed to a cart and towed in darkness through the city streets,

ABOVE: *Portrait of Jacques Alexandre César Charles, who was chosen by the French Academy to put the Montgolfiers' claims to the test, and father of the hydrogen balloon*

Criminals, or animals?

BELOW LEFT: *The first hot-air balloon flight with animal passengers*

BELOW RIGHT: *The landing of the first animal balloonists*

King Louis XVI of France thought balloon flight was far too dangerous for a human passenger, so a basket was used to carry a sheep, a duck, and a cockerel. The Montgolfiers devised an even more powerful smoke-producing formula for the fire, adding old shoes and rotten meat to the straw-and-wool mixture. The smoke and smell this produced drove the royal couple away before they had a chance to inspect the balloon, but within an hour this unpromising fuel had heated enough air to fully inflate the balloon.

After the demonstration flight left the animals unharmed, the Montgolfiers wanted to carry out a manned flight. At first the King refused, because of the dangers involved, but finally agreed that two condemned criminals could make the flight. If they survived, they would be given a free pardon. This was too much for a 26-year-old would-be balloonist named Pilâtre de Rozier, who was determined to be the first man to fly (see page 11).

Lacking enough influence to change the royal mind, he struck a deal with the Marquis d'Arlandes, who also wanted a balloon flight. The Marquis would set to work to persuade the King to let them take the risks, in return for a place aboard the balloon if his persuasion worked. Though Louis gave way in the end, it took a great deal of determined lobbying, including pressure from the Duchesse de Polignac, governess to the royal children, as well as from Queen Marie-Antoinette herself.

RIGHT: *The first hydrogen balloons were difficult to fill, since the gas could only be generated by pouring sulfuric acid on iron filings. Eventually, they settled on generating the gas inside a cask, connected by a pipe to the balloon envelope*

BELOW: *The terrified villagers of Gonesse attack the half-collapsed balloon under the impression it is some hostile monster of the skies*

under an armed escort of both infantry and cavalry. As the torchlit procession passed by, city cab drivers stopped and knelt in the roadway, doffing their hats.

The first hydrogen balloon flight

On the Champ de Mars, preparations took until five in the evening, with the crowd held back by soldiers to ensure that ticket holders had the best view. A cannon was fired, the ropes were released, and the balloon climbed into the sky, through a sudden shower. At 3,000 feet it disappeared into cloud, but through a gap it was seen climbing higher into clearer air, until at last it passed beyond the horizon to the northeast.

Charles's balloon sailed a full 15 miles before descending to earth three-quarters of an hour later in a field on the edge of the village of Gonesse. The terrified villagers reacted violently to the sight of the thrashing envelope, and set upon it with pitchforks, scythes, and muskets, until it was safely cut to pieces. But the event had proved, once and for all, that hydrogen balloons could fly.

Meanwhile, the Montgolfiers' demonstration balloon had been wrecked by a sudden squall, five days before their appointment with the King, the Queen, and the members of the Academy, at the palace of Versailles. Furiously, they worked to produce a smaller replacement, 41 feet across and 57 feet high, and almost spherical in shape. Colored blue and gold and decorated with the royal coat of arms, it was inflated the day before the flight. That night it was taken to the Ministers' Court at Versailles, to be guarded by soldiers and hidden beneath cloths stretched over scaffolding.

The launch was scheduled for one o'clock in the afternoon of the following day, 19 September, 1783, after a celebration banquet. Three timed cannon shots echoed around the courtyard, the ropes were released, and the balloon rose, carrying an animal cargo (see box on page 9). It reached a height of only 1,700 feet, and started losing height after just eight minutes, owing to a split in the fabric—but the demonstration was judged to be highly successful.

First on the scene was an Academy member with the resounding name of François Pilâtre de Rozier, who found that the wicker basket had broken open when falling through the trees—but the sheep and the duck were undamaged and apparently in good spirits. The cockerel was nursing a damaged wing, but an eyewitness claimed to have seen the sheep kicking the cockerel as the balloon started its ascent.

How a hot-air balloon flies

To the official mind, all balloons were the same, and they believed the Montgolfiers too must depend on hydrogen. The brothers knew better, but were still confused over the mysterious gas that sent their balloons skyward, just as smoke and sparks from a fire always soared upward. They decided that the fire must release a different type of gas, which carried the sparks up with it, and which sometimes revealed itself as smoke.

They called it "electric smoke." They decided that only materials that produced a lot of smoke would produce this vital gas to lift the balloon clear of the ground, so they usually settled for a mixture of damp straw and shredded wool. The truth was very different. Heat from the fire simply caused the air to expand, and occupy a greater volume than the same amount of cold air. When the rising column of hot air was diverted to fill the envelope of a balloon, the fully inflated balloon displaced a greater weight of cold air than the weight of the envelope and the hot air it contained. Like the sparks and the smoke, the balloon was bound to sail upward.

The first hot-air manned flight

Clearly, the next step was a balloon to carry human passengers. So they built another balloon of similar size, but with an important difference. It carried its fire with it, in a wrought-iron wire basket slung below the envelope, just above the passenger gallery. Pilâtre de Rozier made a series of tethered test flights, staying aloft up to nine minutes at a time. They tried different fuel formulas, settling for a mixture of straw and rags soaked in spirits of wine. A free ascent was planned for 20 November, from the grounds of the Château La Muette, a Royal residence in the Bois de Boulogne, on the outskirts of the capital, with Pilâtre de Rozier and the Marquis d'Arlandes.

Rumors spread and huge crowds gathered, but once again bad weather postponed the flight. On the morning of the 21st, a tethered flight to test the conditions resulted in the strong wind damaging the envelope, so it very nearly caught fire.

A team of women volunteers worked for two hours to repair the torn panels of fabric and prepare the balloon for flight. During the interval the weather improved, and at last, at six minutes to two on the afternoon of 21 November, the balloon left the ground, free to fly wherever the breeze took it.

The Marquis, struck by the silence of the ascent, looked over the side of the gallery at the faces of the crowd below, then took out a handkerchief and began waving to them. The more practical de Rozier complained they were hardly climbing, and suggested adding more fuel to the fire. With the wind blowing gently from the northwest, they crossed the River Seine and flew across the city streets.

LEFT: *The first Montgolfier to fly carrying human passengers, de Rozier and the Marquis d'Arlandes, 21 November 1783*

By then it was clear that sparks from the fire were burning holes in the envelope. To prevent a disaster, they damped out the fire and the burning fabric with sponges, carried with this kind of emergency in mind. Finally, with the fire safely out and the temperature of the air in the envelope cooling, they began descending gently. They touched down on the present-day site of the Place d'Italie in Paris, after 25 minutes and just over 5 miles; the first manned flight in history.

In the five months since the Montgolfiers' first unmanned flight, the French public had become obsessed by ballooning, and enormous progress had been made. During the intense preparations for de Rozier's and Arlande's historic flight, a rival team had been hard at work on a new man-carrying version of Charles's hydrogen balloon.

Because the hydrogen balloon carried all its gas within it, it had no need of an open neck to collect hot air rising from a fire, and could be made as a perfect sphere. Two valves were fitted to the envelope, which was 27 feet in diameter. One at the bottom allowed the balloon to be inflated, and let gas escape to prevent it from bursting if outside air pressure fell too low at high altitude, or if sunlight heated the envelope to cause the gas inside to expand. Another valve at the top could be opened by pulling a cord running down to the passenger basket, releasing gas to allow the balloon to land.

A special launching stage was built over a drained pond in the garden of the Tuileries Palace in Paris, and the balloon was slung from trees in the nearby Grande Avenue, to be inflated. It was then carried to the launching platform and attached by an elaborate mesh of cables to a wickerwork gondola for the two passengers, Charles himself and one of the Robert brothers, who had helped make the balloon. They also took food, warm clothing, a thermometer and barometer, and a pile of sandbags to act as ballast, to help control the height of the balloon's flight.

BELOW RIGHT: *Ticketless spectators swarm over the wall of the Tuileries Gardens to watch Charles and Robert take off*

BELOW LEFT: *The triumphant ascent of Charles' hydrogen balloon in December 1783, hot on the trail of the Montgolfiers*

Charles's first flight

Finally, on 1 December, the ropes were released, and the balloon flew upward, reaching almost 2,000 feet in the first few minutes. Eyewitnesses claimed half the population of Paris turned up to watch, and they cheered the intrepid pair to the echo. To prolong their flight, Charles and Robert had already started throwing unnecessary items overboard, including surplus blankets and heavy clothing, as the winter sunshine kept them surprisingly warm. Another unexpected blessing was the chance to talk to people on the ground far below as the balloon flight was so quiet.

On and on they flew. After two hours they were approaching the small town of Nesle, when Charles decided to try a landing. He opened the valve in the top of the balloon to make a superbly gentle touchdown, after a journey of 27 miles. They were greeted by a crowd, who helped hold the balloon down. Then three horsemen arrived, having galloped from the Tuileries to see what had happened to the two men.

Charles scribbled a short account of the flight, signed by the local magistrate, to prove the time and distance they had flown. Then, even though darkness had fallen, he set off again on his own. Though the balloon seemed to lose much of its gas on the original flight, this sudden reduction in load meant it climbed even higher than before. Charles rose into sunlight again, and the higher he climbed the colder it grew.

His instruments showed a height of almost 10,000 feet, when pressure changes caused pain in his ears and jaw. He opened the valve at the top of the balloon and started downward again, back into the darkness. Fortunately, the moon had risen, giving him a clear view of the ground, and once again he made a gentle landing just three miles away from his previous touchdown, after a second flight of 35 minutes.

Charles never flew again, but, on that single day, his hydrogen balloon had all but banished the Montgolfiers' hot-air flights to the pages of history. Although they planned larger and more spectacular flights, and although hot-air balloons could be inflated far more quickly than hydrogen balloons, their range was limited. Even if they could take enough fuel with them to stay aloft for hours, the problem of sparks burning holes in the envelope was not only appallingly dangerous while flying, but the resulting damage meant that, all too often, a new flight meant that a new balloon was needed.

Balloons over England

While the whole craze for ballooning had initially been confined to France, the fashion soon spread overseas. In the following year, Montgolfier hot-air balloons flew in Italy and England, but many other projects failed because of lack of money. Finally, an Italian named Vincenzo Lunardi, a clerk at the Neapolitan Embassy in London, launched a subscription scheme in July 1784 to finance a hydrogen balloon flight to be made from the grounds of London's Chelsea Royal Hospital.

By the middle of August the balloon had been completed, filled with air, and hung at London's Lyceum—a hall that eventually became the famous theater— for the public to admire. It was similar to

TOP: *After landing at Nesle, Charles takes off alone for his second flight, watched by de Rozier and companions, who had ridden from Paris to follow the balloon's progress*

ABOVE: *Vincenzo Lunardi, the first ballonist to fly over England, with his cherished pet cat*

Charles's successful design but lacked the valve at the top of the balloon to make landing easier and safer, though it had a much smaller, simpler, and lighter basket to carry the passengers. In the meantime, the disappointed London crowds had rioted when two other hot-air balloons caught fire and were destroyed before they had the chance to take-off.

This caused the authorities to ban Lunardi's flight from the Chelsea Royal Hospital. He then arranged to use the training ground of the Honourable Artillery Company at Moorfields in London, but, when he tried to collect the balloon from the Lyceum, the proprietor refused to release it unless he was paid a share of the public subscriptions that had been raised to meet the costs of the flight.

Poor Lunardi told the Honourable Artillery Company he would not be able to make the flight on the planned date of 15 September after all, and they demanded a 100-guinea ($168) cancellation fee, failing which they would throw his generating apparatus off their land forthwith.

Fortunately, two of Lunardi's friends bought off the artillerymen, and Lunardi obtained a police warrant for the release of his balloon from the Lyceum. A posse of constables collected it, and the balloon was taken under guard to Moorfields the day before the launch. Filling went on all that night, though when the man in charge returned after a few hours' sleep at four in the morning he found the crew drunk and no more gas had entered the envelope since midnight.

This meant the balloon was still only partly inflated by early afternoon. The mood of the crowd—distracted by the rumored escape of a mad bullock, the actual collapse of a stand, the ducking of a pickpocket, and a battle with passengers whose coaches had arrived late and blocked the view—was

turning angry and impatient. It was approaching 2 o'clock when Lunardi realized it was now or never. Having persuaded his passenger to remain behind, he set off in the partially-inflated balloon, with only a cat, a dog, and a caged pigeon for company, but liberal stocks of food and wine.

Lunardi's balloon drifted northward, while he feasted on cold chicken and wine. As his cat suffered from the cold, he floated to earth to release it after an hour and a half. He then took off again by throwing overboard his empty wine bottle, his cutlery, and all his ballast bags. After 35 minutes he landed at the village of Standon, more than 20 miles north of his starting point, where a monument records his epic flight.

Lunardi was presented at Court, while his balloon, his dog, and his cat were put on public show in Oxford Street, London, and he was the toast of London society. But his subsequent flights were less successful, as the impatience of the watching crowds often led to take-offs in poor weather. At last, on a take-off from Newcastle-upon-Tyne in the northeast of England, several of the ground crew let go of the ropes before the arranged signal. This left a young man named Ralph Heron still clutching his rope as the balloon shot skyward, carrying him with it. Eventually he fell, and died soon afterwards. The people who had praised Lunardi so extravagantly now turned against him, and he left England forever.

Less than three weeks after Lunardi's first ascent, an Englishman named James Sadler made his first hot-air balloon flight. After that, he too switched to hydrogen balloons, and made some spectacular flights in strong winds. Unfortunately, this resulted in some violent landings, and, on one flight, the balloon dragged him five miles across country before he fell out of the basket, and it took off again without him, never to be seen again. Sadler, however, would return to the skies.

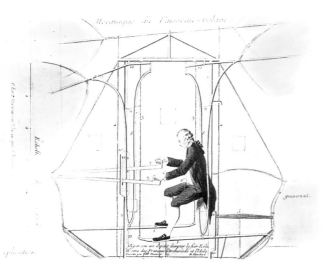

ABOVE: *Blanchard's unsuccessful pedal-powered flying machine was designed to be able to fly into the wind*

RIGHT: *Blanchard later fitted rudders and paddles to allow him to steer his balloon, also without success*

Crossing the English Channel

At least landings were possible at the end of all these early flights, as they had taken place over dry land. One man who set out to change all this was a ferociously ambitious Frenchman named Jean-Pierre Blanchard. He had invented a crude bicycle in 1769, but then tried to extend his talents to producing a pedal-powered flying machine. Refusing to let facts interfere with a good story, he claimed to have flown at a height of 80 feet, and at an amazing speed of 75 m.p.h. Blanchard also claimed to have invented a parachute, and to have made two successful jumps, but there is little doubt these two claims were as false as the flying machine.

What Blanchard *did* was make his first flight in a hydrogen balloon from the Champ de Mars in Paris on 2 March 1784. He also flew from Rouen, and from Bordeaux, but the French ballooning scene was now so crowded, there was little chance of winning the fame he sought so desperately. In August 1784 he moved to the more promising surroundings of London, where a man with his own balloon could find many wealthy patrons willing to pay handsomely for the chance of a flight (see box on page 17).

Blanchard's most spectacular exploit was an attempt to cross the English Channel to his native France, sponsored by Dr John Jeffries, an American with a practice in London. They took off on the morning of 7 January 1785. Although they dropped all their ballast overboard by the time the French coast was but a few miles away, the balloon never climbed to a safe altitude, and it seemed they would come down in the sea. Frantically, the two men began jettisoning everything they could.

First to go were the extravagant gondola decorations, followed by Blanchard's steering gear. Then followed the anchors, the two men's coats, and then their trousers. The remedy worked when they were skimming the waves, and the balloon climbed higher than ever before, to cross the French coast and finally deposit its passengers safely on earth 12 miles inland, in the Forest of Felmores, dressed only in their underwear. It was a splendid achievement. Blanchard was given a prize by Louis XVI and a life pension, but Jeffries had to be content with the glory alone.

Blanchard used his new-found means to set up a ballooning school in London. After one flight, he claimed to have returned precisely to his starting point, to prove his skill at balloon flying. In fact the balloon had landed some way away, and had been towed back to the start by two horsemen. He made other equally untrue claims, and in the end a disappointed crowd wrecked the school.

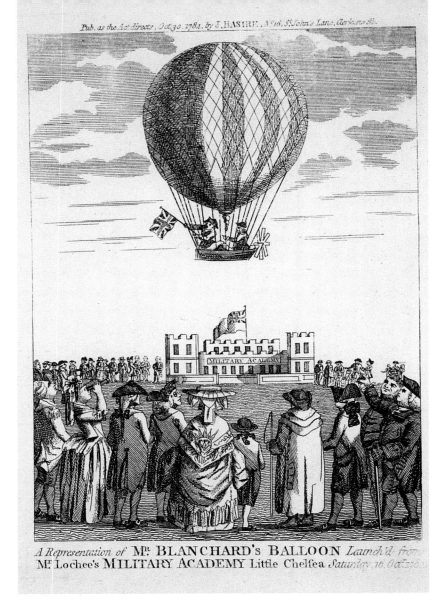

A Representation of Mr. BLANCHARD's BALLOON Launch'd from Mr Lochee's MILITARY ACADEMY Little Chelsea Saturday 16 Oct

Blanchard's thirst for glory

ABOVE LEFT: *Blanchard takes off on a London demonstration flight from the grounds of the Royal Military Academy, Chelsea*

ABOVE RIGHT: *Dr John Jeffries, backer and copilot for Blanchard's cross-Channel flight*

Blanchard treated his benefactors extremely badly. When Dr John Sheldon paid for a flight, to carry himself and his scientific instruments, Blanchard threw the equipment out to enable the balloon to climb more quickly. Another scientific traveler, a Boston-born American named Dr John Jeffries who had qualified in England, and who was interested in meteorology, managed to complete a flight with Blanchard without having his possessions thrown overboard, and undertook to pay the costs of a balloon flight across the English Channel to France.

In Blanchard's eyes, this generosity was no guarantee that the doctor would actually be able to take part in the flight, and share the glory. In December 1784 he took his balloon to coastal Dover, but succeeded in barricading himself inside Dover Castle and locking Jeffries out. The resourceful Jeffries recruited a squad of sailors as extra muscle, and then enlisted the services of the castle governor to negotiate an agreement between the two balloonists.

Nevertheless, Blanchard was far from finished. When the inflated balloon—carrying a gondola packed with Blanchard's own steering gear, consisting of wing paddles and a hand-turned fan to act as a propeller—was tested for lift with the two men aboard, it was found to be too heavy to take off. Blanchard generously offered to make the flight alone, but Jeffries was suspicious enough to inspect the Frenchman's clothing, only to find he was wearing a leather belt under his coat—with a set of heavy lead weights!

ABOVE: *Jean-Pierre Blanchard, "The Aeronaut"– brave, but entirely dedicated to his own personal glory*

Blanchard then moved back to France, and went on to make a series of flights all over Europe, two of them in a hot-air balloon, but the rest in hydrogen balloons. After the outbreak of the French Revolution, Blanchard was arrested in Austria on a charge of distributing pro-Revolutionary literature. He escaped to America in time to make the first balloon flight from American soil at Philadelphia on 9 January 1793. Ironically, his old comrade Jeffries was then only a few hundred miles away. After practicing medicine in London for ten years, Jeffries returned to Boston in 1789.

Death of Pilâtre de Rozier

Blanchard's Channel crossing beat another renowned balloonist to the post. Pilâtre de Rozier had already been working on an attempt to cross the English Channel from France to England at the time, on what he had promised his young English fiancée would be his last flight. He found backers for his enterprise, but, for such an experienced balloonist, the design of his craft seemed bizarre.

Whereas all other balloonists had flown with either a hot-air or hydrogen balloon on any given ascent, de Rozier was to fly a mushroom-shaped hybrid more than 60 feet tall, with both elements in its construction. There is evidence that the experienced de Rozier himself was deeply concerned at the balloon's radical design, which may have originated with his sponsors. But the idea of placing a spherical hydrogen balloon on top of a cylindrical envelope, which would be filled with hot air from an airborne furnace burning bundles of wood and charcoal, seemed a recipe for disaster.

The flight was to start from Boulogne, which meant waiting for weeks for a south or southeasterly wind to replace the prevailing westerlies, and blow the balloon across the narrowest part of the Channel. At last, on the morning of 15 June 1785, more than five months after Blanchard and Jeffries' flight, conditions seemed favorable. With de Rozier and Jules Romain, maker of the balloon, on board, the giant mushroom rose into the sky. It drifted northward and rose to a height of some 5,000 feet and then drifted slowly back over the coast.

Then the almost inevitable happened. The tall and cumbersome balloon caught fire and came plunging back to earth not far from its starting point. De Rozier was killed in the impact, and Romain died within minutes. Each witness of the disaster had a slightly different story to tell, but it seemed likely the problem began with de Rozier having to vent gas from the top of the hydrogen balloon, to reduce excess pressure caused by the heat of the Montgolfier balloon below it. Because fire damage was limited to the top of the balloon, where the gas escaped, this was more likely to have been triggered by a spark of static electricity, than by the furnace 60 feet below. Once the hydrogen had burned and escaped, the balloon lost almost all its lift, and the crash was inevitable.

TOP: *The inevitable happens—the hydrogen ignites and the blazing balloon loses lift, plunging de Rozier and Romain to their deaths*

ABOVE: *François Pilâtre de Rozier, first man to fly and later the first to die in an air accident*

Across the Irish Sea

Yet ballooning was now firmly established, and intrepid fliers were now challenging even wider and more dangerous water barriers. A whole series of unsuccessful attempts had been made to cross the Irish Sea from west to east, before James Sadler returned to ballooning, after his earlier punishing experiences. In spite of dropping into the Bristol Channel on one flight, and being blown more than a hundred miles in a gale on another, in 1812 he decided to build a balloon to cross the Irish Sea.

Shrewdly, he made the balloon a large one, 55 feet in diameter. It was only partially inflated, to allow for expansion as it climbed. He carried more than half a ton of ballast and he set off alone on 1 October, in a brisk southwesterly. At one stage, the balloon sprang a leak, but Sadler climbed up and repaired it with the aid of his neckcloth.

After more than four hours, the balloon drifted across the isle of Anglesey, off the coast of North Wales. Sadler changed height, hoping to drift toward Liverpool, but was blown out to sea instead. Eventually, he had to land on the water, to be rescued by a trawler. It was a heart-breakingly narrow failure, but his younger son Windham would make the first successful crossing of the Irish Sea almost five years later, landing in Anglesey after a remarkably straightforward flight of five and a half hours.

Yet the Sadlers' triumph was short-lived. Windham Sadler died in 1824, when his balloon hit a chimney stack when attempting to land from a flight in Lancashire. It was seven years after his triumphant sea crossing, and he was still only 28. For all the skill and courage of this new professional breed of aeronauts, the sky was still a cruel and unforgiving place. But the achievements of these fragile and temperamental craft were only just beginning.

ABOVE: *James Sadler takes off on his heroic and almost successful attempt to cross the Irish Sea in 1812*

Tales of the unsuccessful

ABOVE RIGHT: *The Itinerant Aeronaut, a cartoon which satirized the wanderings of balloonists like Blanchard from country to country, to find new public backing for their flights*

If Pilâtre de Rozier's Channel attempt had been tragedy, later ventures to cross the much wider Irish Sea became pure farce. First of all, just two days after de Rozier's fatal ascent, another Frenchman, a Dr Potain who lived in Dublin, set out to float across from Ireland to Wales on the westerly wind. Despite a gondola equipped with paddles, rudder, and propeller, the balloon was blown back over the land, coming down at Powerstock, a dozen miles south of the city.

The next attempt was made by two men, the heavily-built Richard Crosbie and a young army officer named Richard McGuire. When the balloon was inflated, the two men found they were too heavy for it to take off. Crosbie pushed McGuire out of the basket, but the balloon was still too heavy. The two men changed places, but the balloon still refused to move.

Crosbie pushed McGuire out again, and had more gas piped into the balloon while he waited alongside. As soon as the balloon showed signs of lifting, McGuire leapt aboard before the amazed Crosbie, and it shot upward like a cork, only narrowly missing a nearby chimneystack.

The balloon headed out across the coast, but the attempts to persuade it to take off had overinflated it with hydrogen, and, as it rose higher, the pressure of gas within the envelope increased, until finally it ruptured, some nine miles out to sea. When the basket plunged into the waves, McGuire was thrown out, and, relieved of his weight, the semi-inflated balloon rose again with the young army officer hanging upside down with his ankle entwined in a coil of rope.

He finally managed to struggle free, and after swimming for half an

hour was rescued by boat. He was taken back to Ireland, only to be given a knighthood by the Lord Lieutenant! Finally, Crosbie tried again, on his own, two months later, but he too came down in the sea, and was rescued by ship. After that the sea remained uncrossed for 27 years, until James Sadler made his valiant attempt in 1812.

2. Higher, Faster, Farther . . .

ABOVE: *Balloons everywhere: an early nineteenth-century cartoon mocks the mania for balloons as fashion icons*

RIGHT: *The French dream of a balloon invasion of England, aided in this picture by winds which blow from opposite directions at the start and end of the journey*

As the casualty list among the early balloonists seemed to be lengthening, the public interest in them began to falter. People, particularly in France, began to see the balloon as little more than a dangerous and disappointing curiosity, though a few were able to see its future potential.

Benjamin Franklin, asked what was the use of a balloon, summed it up in his famous reply, "What use is a new-born baby?" Nevertheless, Franklin was living and working in Paris, and had seen the lighter-than-air revolution at first hand. His countrymen back home were much slower to take to the skies themselves, or even show much interest in those who did.

Following Blanchard's first Philadelphia flight, ballooning was painfully slow to catch the public interest in North America. Even when an American aeronaut took to the air, such as the showman Rufus Wells, much of his flying was done overseas. He used a succession of hot-air and hydrogen balloons on ascents in Europe, Egypt, India, Java, Japan, Australia, and even South America. Those of his fellow countrymen, like John La Mountain, Thaddeus Lowe, and John Wise, who did most of their flying in American skies, were examples of a new breed of balloonists; showmen rather than explorers.

Part of the problem was that, after the first flush of excitement as flight became possible, the public had begun to realize the limitations of the balloon. Once the claims of aeronauts like Blanchard to be able to steer

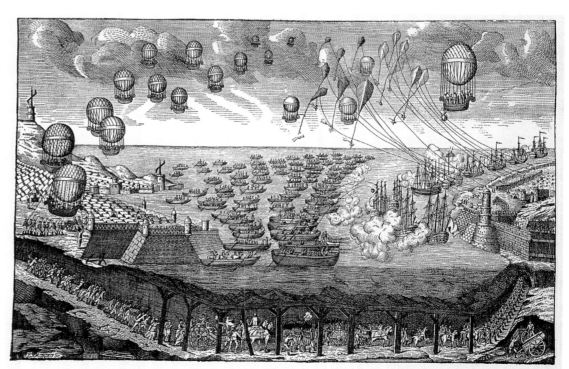

A PROJECTED INVASION OF ENGLAND.

The above is the reproduction of an old print published in France in 1803, which shows that the idea of boring a tunnel under the Channel originated as far back as the beginning of the century. The scene represents a project for the invasion of England by subterranean and other means. Among other quaint absurdities, the wind carries the balloons from left to right, whilst it also supports the kites by blowing in the opposite direction !

207

The BATTLE
of the
BALLOONS.
Published as the Act directs

Behold an odd Fight, two odd Nations between,
Such odd Fighting as this was never yet feen: —

But fuch Fights will be common (as Dunce to feel Rod)
In the Year of OneThoufand eight Hundred and odd.

Printed for & Sold by Bowles & Carver.   *No69 in St Pauls Church Yard, London.*

his craft by oars, paddles, fans, and windmills were shown to be totally false, it became clear that the balloon offered very little as a serious form of transport.

The Montgolfiers' fond dream of a massed force of balloons to carry troops across the Channel for a successful invasion of England remained a fantasy, though shrewder military minds such as the Emperor Napoleon hoped that such a thing might still be possible. Yet the experiences of those who tried to make sea crossings using prevailing winds showed that even these were fickle and dangerous as a way of predicting one's destination.

Balloons and show business

What happened instead was that ballooning became a spectacle for entertainment rather than a new and expanding science. At one level, every circus acrobat was tempted to include a balloon in the act. Thanks to a range of cheap and simple hot-air balloons mass-produced by the French partnership of Lartet and Kirsch, they were able to fly as the very first Montgolfiers did, using heat from a fire on the ground to keep their balloon aloft for the duration of their act.

However, as balloons became more familiar, the objectives of the leading balloonists became more ambitious and more dangerous. Night flights proved to be one way of keeping the public interested, and a Frenchman called Tétu-Brissy made the first night ascent as early as June 1786 when he took off from Paris and survived eleven hours in the air, including a severe storm.

As balloons became larger, and provided more lift, the next fashion was to carry animals as additional passengers. Tétu-Brissy himself made two flights on horseback, with the animal standing patiently on a platform slung below the envelope of the balloon.

TOP LEFT: *The Battle of the Balloons: a futuristic view of aerial fighting between groups of armed balloons*

TOP RIGHT: *A fanciful idea for an armed balloon, though the gun seems too large (and inadequately supported), while the lifting balloons are far too small*

ABOVE: *An even more ambitious idea for an aerial ship, with every kind of convenience, including privies and liquor storage slung below the hull*

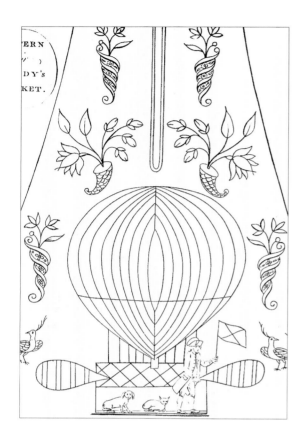

ABOVE LEFT: *Ladies' embroidery pattern for a pocket motif of a hydrogen balloon, complete with steering paddles*

ABOVE RIGHT: *The death of English balloonist Thomas Harris when his escape valve worked all too well on its first trial. His lady companion, lying unconscious at the left of the picture, managed to survive the accident*

This was too tame for some other balloonists, who added to the sense of danger that ballooning still inspired in their audiences, by carrying larger and more lethal—and wild—animals into the air with them on their flights. But, as a source of peril, this was far eclipsed by the spreading fashion for fireworks, to be carried in the gondola and launched into the night sky as the balloon rose. Although night flying had its advantages, since the air tended to be more stable in good weather, the idea of carrying naked flames below a hydrogen balloon seemed a recipe for disaster.

Sure enough, a series of spectacular accidents, involving fliers as illustrious as Madame Blanchard (see box on page 25) underlined the dangers in unmistakable fashion. Unfortunately, these disasters tended to obscure the reality that balloons were becoming progressively safer. A series of clever inventions, in design and equipment, was beginning to make them easier to control and more reliable by far.

Inventions and improvements

One of the most important of these inventions was a device for bringing the balloon back to earth more quickly while landing. Though the English balloonist Thomas Harris had devised a large valve for expelling the gas and keeping the balloon on the ground once it touched down, he suffered a fatal accident on the first test flight. Nevertheless the principle was sound, and the American balloonist Professor John Wise achieved it in a different way by the invention of the "rip cord," which, instead of opening a valve, tore open a special panel in the top of the balloon to achieve instant deflation, and keep the balloon firmly on the ground after landing with no chance of a second take-off.

Another improvement made ballooning much cheaper. Hydrogen was expensive, and inflating the balloon was difficult, but by the early years of the nineteenth century the spread of gas lighting offered balloonists an alternative. Using coal gas instead of hydrogen meant that a balloon could be inflated simply by connecting it to a gas main, and coal gas was a great deal cheaper. There was only one drawback. It produced less lift than the same amount of the more costly hydrogen, so that, to ascend with a particular load, a coal-gas balloon had to be much larger than one filled with pure hydrogen.

Even this was balanced by a compensating advantage. Coal gas was far less sensitive to temperature changes than hydrogen. Where a hydrogen balloon might rise or fall quite sharply as it flew through a mixture of cloudy and sunny conditions, a balloon filled with coal gas would fly more smoothly, and stay aloft for much longer.

Monsieur Garnerin and Madame Blanchard

André Jacques Garnerin was a keen balloonist who was overtaken by war and revolution, after making his first flight from Metz in 1787. Conscripted into the army of Revolutionary France, he was taken prisoner by the British and then transferred to a fortress in Hungary, where he dreamed of escape by the newly-invented parachute. After being released three years later, he succeeded in making a balloon flight in October 1797, carrying with him a vast, umbrella-shaped parachute some 30 feet across. At a height of some 3,000 feet, Garnerin stepped out of the balloon and took to his parachute.

It worked—just. Because the huge umbrella had no gap to allow the wind to escape in a controlled and stable descent, the terrified Garnerin came to earth in a series of wild swings, but survived the experience. Five years later he repeated his feat over London, descending from 10,000 feet in an even more violent progression, but once again living to tell the tale. In time, his experiences led to improved parachutes, and both his wife and niece became able parachutists in their own right.

Garnerin's growing reputation was stopped in its tracks by an ambitious attempt to honor the newly-crowned Emperor Napoleon. He produced a huge, unmanned hydrogen balloon decorated with a ceremonial inscription and carrying a huge gilded crown and a set of colored lanterns. Released at the height of the celebrations, the vast sphere sailed off into the darkness and all seemed well.

Unfortunately, Garnerin's balloon showed up the next morning over Rome, causing alarm among the public. It skimmed the city rooftops

ABOVE: *Madame Blanchard, in one of the tiny gondolas which became her trademark*

and eventually disappeared into a nearby lake, but not before leaving part of its golden crown on the tomb of the Emperor Nero. The symbolism was tailor-made for the press, and Garnerin fell from favor. For the time being, official balloon events in France passed into the hands of Madame Blanchard, wife of the famous Jean-Pierre Blanchard.

Madame Blanchard courted danger with every flight. Not only did she specialize in balloons that had gondolas so small and fragile they were perilous in themselves, but she organized ever more spectacular displays of fireworks. Part of her act was to shower the crowd below with bombs supported on miniature parachutes, drenching them in showers of colored sparks. Unfortunately, it was Madame Blanchard who needed the parachute when, on 7 July 1819, the torch she was using to light the fireworks ignited hydrogen which was escaping from the balloon.

First she tried to put out the fire. Then, as the balloon started to plunge toward the ground, she threw out all the ballast to slow down the descent. The rush of her fall seemed to put out the flames, but the balloon hit the rooftops, and the tiny gondola was overturned as it hit a chimney stack. Losing her grip, Madame Blanchard fell to her death on the roadway below.

VUE DE LA VILLE DE LYON

MACHINE AËROSTATIQUE

De Cent vingt pieds de hauteur sur cent de Diametre construite à Lyon, avec une enveloppe formée par trois papiers entre deux Canevas, et un filet qui en enveloppe le tour et retenoit la Gallerie sur la surface choisi y represente diver allegorie. Cette Machine, faite sous la direction de M.e de Montgolfier l'ainé au vœu d'une Inscription, s'est elevée le 19 Janvier 1784 à prés de 3 mille cinq cent pieds de hauteur, portant avec elle M. de Montgolfier l'ainé, M. Pilatre de Rozier, M. le Prince Char.les de Ligne, M. le Comte de la Porte d'Anglefort, M. le Comte de Laurencin, M. le Comte de Dampierre et M. Fontaine de Lyon celé Coöperateur. Sa direction fut verticale et parvint à sa plus grande hauteur en 25 minutes de tems, alors s'étant fait une déchirure à l'enveloppe, cette Machine redit au course Sa monture, et descendit insensi.lement et en promptement dans une prairie aux environs de Lyon, sans qu'aucun des nouveaux argonautes eut éprouvé la moindre incommodité; Jamais scene ne fut plus touchante que l'accueil et les acclamations qui furent faites aux Voyageurs, et sur tout les embrassemens reiterées du Prince de Ligne et de son Fils. Le Soir à la Comedie il fut rendu une Cantate à l'honneur de M. de Montgolfier qui fut couronné en ve se Comptoienne de Voyage dans la Loge de Elisandance. Tous les habitans de la Ville de Lyon et plus de 3 mille Etrangers qu'y étoient venus furent tenoins de cette belle experience.

ABOVE: *Green's splendid* Royal Vauxhall *balloon, which made more than 500 successful flights, allowing Green to take aloft thousands of enthusiasts, among them the Victorian writer Henry Mayhew. Green eventually retired to Aerial House in Highgate, London, where he died of heart failure at 85*

LEFT: *The largest Montgolfier ever made rang down the curtain on the hot-air balloon which first took human beings aloft. For the future belonged, it seemed, to the hydrogen balloon*

The first flight in a coal-gas balloon was made by the English balloonist Charles Green on 19 July 1821 from London's Green Park to celebrate the crowning of King George IV. Green reached a height of 11,000 feet and though he had some hair-raising escapes—including one that resulted from the sabotage of one of his balloons by cutting the lines that supported the gondola—he made more than 200 flights over the course of the next 14 years.

Green and the Royal Vauxhall balloon

He then came to an arrangement with the owners of London's Vauxhall pleasure gardens to build a much larger balloon, called the *Royal Vauxhall*. This was made from the finest Italian silk in alternating strips of red and white, glued together rather than stitched. It had a capacity of 70,000 cubic feet and stood 80 feet high from the bottom of the gondola to the top of the balloon. This gave the balloon enormous lifting power, and on its first ascent, on 9 September 1836, it took a ton of ballast, 36 policemen, and 20 laborers to hold it down, until the passengers climbed aboard.

Even then, with nine people and 450 pounds of ballast on board, it rocketed skyward when released. Furiously, Green operated the valves to dump more than 20 percent of the balloon's gas to reduce the rate of climb, but even so it reached an altitude of 13,000 feet in five minutes, which is a respectable rate of ascent for a modern aircraft.

To keep this vast power under control, Green had devised the "trail rope." This was a cable 1,000 feet long, which trailed from the gondola. When the balloon was less than a thousand feet high, part of the rope trailed on the ground, relieving the balloon of part of its weight. If the balloon started to climb, it lifted more of the rope clear of the ground and had to support more of its weight. If it lost altitude, more of the rope trailed on the ground and weight was reduced.

The result of this was a damping effect which helped regulate the height of the balloon without the need to release gas from the envelope or use up valuable ballast. Not only did it make flight smoother and safer, in the long run it would almost certainly increase the balloon's range, and Green went on to fit the rope with a set of copper floats to allow it to be used when crossing the sea.

ABOVE: *Charles Green's long list of successful flights helped to develop safer and more controllable balloons*

The Grahams

The English balloonists George Graham and his wife deserve a prize as the most accident-prone of all the early fliers. George's first flight in August 1823 was a failure because the fabric of the balloon was not gas-tight, so it refused to take off and a riot broke out. His second leaked so much gas that it lifted him into the air and dropped him in a flooded gravel pit only a few hundred yards away. When he flew from Plymouth he came down in the waters of Plymouth Sound.

Mrs Graham was scarcely more successful than her unlucky husband. In August 1836 she flew from the west side of London with the mad Duke of Brunswick as her passenger. The balloon sailed across the city and finally landed at Brentwood to the east. Before the balloon could be secured, the Duke jumped out, and the balloon took off again. Mrs Graham was caught off balance and fell out of the gondola.

June 1838 was the month of the coronation of Queen Victoria, and to celebrate the event both Grahams made a flight from Green Park, close to London's Buckingham Palace. They knocked a stone off a house roof, which killed an unfortunate passer-by and blighted the event.

In 1851 they celebrated the Great Exhibition by almost colliding with the Crystal Palace exhibition hall just after take-off. They flew low over London until they collided with the roof of a house belonging to a Colonel North in Piccadilly, so violently that they were both knocked unconscious and fell out of the balloon, which drifted off on its own. The two intrepid aeronauts were found later on the roof, with no apparent explanation of how they arrived there.

Crossing the Atlantic

So confident was Green of the potential of his large, long-distance balloon, especially after the Nassau flight (see box on page 30), that he proposed making a flight across the Atlantic from east to west, against the prevailing winds. He intended adding a series of canvas buckets fitted with retaining valves to his trail rope, to allow him to fly at low altitude over the sea and pick up extra water ballast on his voyage. He also devised a clockwork propeller to enable the balloon to be driven against the wind, but severe injuries after a crash in a gale meant the project was never put into action.

Several years previously, on 9 September 1830, the first American balloonist, Professor Charles Ferson Durant, had made a flight from the Castle Garden in New York. So Green's ideas struck a chord among US followers of the sport, about the much more practical idea of riding the prevailing westerlies from North America to Europe.

Though American readers had been astonished to read in the pages of the *New York Daily News* that one of Green's collaborators, Monck Mason, had landed in South Carolina after spending three days crossing the ocean from Britain in April 1844, it was later revealed to be a hoax concocted by the American writer Edgar Allen Poe. By then, several American balloonists had tried raising sufficient cash to finance eastbound crossings, but none had managed to raise enough to make a serious attempt.

The first real Atlantic challenge was mounted by a wealthy sportsman named O. A. Gager, who financed a balloon called, appropriately, the *Atlantic*. With a capacity of 50,000 cubic feet it carried a gondola with a lifeboat slung beneath it, in case the crew had to ditch in the sea. He signed up Professors Wise and La Mountain, and the three of them, with a newspaper reporter, set off on a test flight from St Louis in 1859, carrying a sack of airmail letters and packages.

Carried on a brisk southwesterly gale, they headed across Illinois, Iowa, and Ohio until they found themselves being blown across Lake Erie at the height of the storm, with the balloon losing height. Putting their faith in the sky rather than the water, they cut the lifeboat adrift to reduce the weight, and even threw the mail overboard to gain height. The tactic worked, and the balloon climbed away to safety, finally coming to earth close to the northern border of New York state after a flight of 809 miles which lasted 10 minutes short of 20 hours.

Royal Gardens, Vauxhall.

ASCENT

OF

THE ROYAL

NASSAU BALLOON

FOR THE

Benefit of the Widow

OF

The late Mr. COCKING,

NEXT WEDNESDAY,

9th AUGUST, 1837.

The Friends and Relations of Mrs. COCKING most respectfully acquaint the Nobility, Gentry, and Public, that the Proprietors of Vauxhall having most kindly granted the Gardens and the use of their Royal Nassau Balloon for the above purpose, and Mr. Green having, also, most generously offered his valuable services, an Ascent will take place Next Wednesday, August 9, when all the Proceeds will be appropriated to the relief of the unfortunate Widow, who is entirely left without the means of support.

Seats in the Car may be secured on application at the Gardens; Gentlemen, £21.---Ladies, £10 : 10s.
☞ Doors open at HALF-PAST TWO.   Balloon to start at SIX.
Admission, HALF-A-CROWN.

ABOVE: *Green's balloon was later renamed the* Nassau *(see box on page 30) in honor of an epic journey across Northern Europe: this poster advertises a flight to raise funds for the widow of Robert Cocking, another airborne pioneer who was killed while demonstrating a parachute*

FAR LEFT: *Poster advertising one of Green's night flights in the Royal Vauxhall balloon*

The largest balloon of all

In spite of this promising start, the *Atlantic* never tried the ocean crossing, but already Professor Lowe was at work on a rival balloon. This was even larger and more ambitious, the biggest hydrogen balloon yet designed, fully 200 feet high when completely inflated with 725,000 cubic feet of gas. Made from 6,000 yards of twilled muslin, the *City of New York* (later renamed the *Great Western*) created a designed lift of 22.5 tons, enough to support a closed wickerwork gondola and no mere lifeboat in case of accident, but a 30-foot steam launch named *Leonine*, after Professor Lowe's wife.

ABOVE: *The* Great Western, *only partly inflated with coal gas, rises from the grounds of the Crystal Palace in New York City*

Clearly, inflating this enormous balloon was no easy undertaking. In November 1859, it was taken to the Crystal Palace at the junction of Fifth Avenue and Forty-second Street in New York, and connected to a main of the New York Gas Company. Sadly, the enormous balloon took all the gas the company could deliver, but remained only partly inflated. Lowe then had the balloon hauled all the way to Philadelphia, and connected to the mains of the Point Breeze Gas Works, but the attempt was postponed with the onset of winter.

Not until June 1860 was the huge balloon—originally named *City of New York* and, after its move to Philadelphia, retitled the *Great Western*—fully inflated and able to take off on a test flight. As with the smaller *Atlantic*, all went well, and the signs seemed encouraging. But three months later, on 8 September, when the balloon was being inflated again ready for the ocean crossing, a sudden squall seized the partly filled balloon and tore the envelope to pieces. Lowe immediately began working on a new balloon to make the crossing, but once again was overtaken by changes in the weather, and the effects of the approaching Civil War (see box on page 34).

The Flight of the *Nassau*

Charles Green's *Royal Vauxhall* balloon left on its most famous flight from London's Vauxhall Gardens on the afternoon of 7 November 1836, with a crew of three, a 1,000-foot trail rope, more than 120 pounds of fine foods, six gallons of sherry, port, and brandy, and a specially-designed coffee pot which could be heated by quicklime.

At first the balloon sailed southeast over the county of Kent, before swinging to the east and heading for the wide waters of the North Sea.

By throwing out a small proportion of their 450 pounds of ballast, they were able to gain height and pick up a more favorable air current, which swung them back toward the Channel and the French coast, which they crossed near Calais.

As darkness fell they lit their safety lamp and dined in style as the balloon sailed on over northern France. As they crossed the Belgian border near Liège, they could see the fires of iron works and furnaces hard at work below, but, after that, total darkness overcame them. As dawn approached, they dropped more ballast, and witnessed the sun appearing over the horizon from a height of 12,000 feet.

Though they could plainly see a countryside of rolling hills below, some of them covered in snow, they had no idea of their position. They decided to land, but found that, as they approached the ground, contrary winds forced them to throw out more ballast and climb away again for safety. Only at their third attempt did they manage to touch down on the edge of a wood. It was 7.30 in the morning, and local countrymen told them they had reached the German duchy of Nassau after an epic if comfortable flight of 480 miles—the longest balloon flight so far achieved.

They were taken with their balloon to the nearby town of Weilburg, where they were entertained to a series of concerts, balls, and banquets. These included an elaborate christening ceremony when the balloon, inflated with air for the occasion, was renamed the *Great Balloon of Nassau*. The balloonists and their craft later returned to England, but in all its later flights Green's record-breaking balloon flew under its new name of *Nassau*.

Nadar and *Le Géant*

Meanwhile another huge balloon was taking to the skies of Europe. Unlike the American balloons, this was not made with an ocean crossing in mind, but with the more commercial objective of raising funds for its creator's experiments with heavier-than-air flight. This was a pioneer photographer, Félix Tournachon, who traded under the name "Nadar." His balloon, named appropriately *Le Géant*, was assembled from 22,000 yards of the finest white silk, and enclosed 212,000 cubic feet of gas.

Though it stood 196 feet high, it provided only a fraction of the lift of the American balloons. However, this was enough for a huge basketwork gondola like a small house, enclosing stores, cabins, a bathroom, a photographic darkroom, and even a printing press, with a flat roof providing a balcony on which the passengers could take the air. When the balloon took off on its first test flight from Paris on 4 October 1863, it carried 15 people, and came down just 15 miles east of the city, in a spectacularly rough landing which resulted in the gondola and passengers being dragged for half a mile across country.

Two weeks later, *Le Géant* took off again on a more ambitious flight, with nine aboard. As the vast balloon sailed into the dusk, the passengers dined on the flat-roof balcony of the gondola and admired

ABOVE: **Le Géant** *comes down to earth in north-west Germany, crowning a spectacular flight with an even more spectacular landing*

the sunset. The winds took them north and east into the gathering darkness, and by dawn the balloon was crossing Holland, with the prospect of drifting over the North Sea. Fortunately, the wind veered to carry the balloon to the east, across northern Germany, and, when approaching the city of Hanover, Nadar decided to bring the monster back down to earth.

Unfortunately, the wind that had carried them for more than 400 miles was still blowing hard at ground level, and the landing was fearsomely rough. The huge gondola was dragged across the countryside by the partly deflated balloon at a horrific speed, tearing away branches and even small trees, and shedding passengers along the way.

At one point an approaching train had to screw down the brakes and come to a shuddering halt just in time, as balloon and gondola plowed across the tracks. When it finally came to rest, only Madame Nadar remained aboard. The rest had been scattered across country, with a variety of injuries.

ABOVE: *The Battle of Fleurus, where the French won a decisive victory over the Austrians in 1794, thanks to the first use of an observation balloon*

Balloons go to war

Though huge balloons continued to be made, and to fly, in Europe, in the United States balloonists had sterner duties to carry out. The outbreak of the Civil War meant that the unrivaled views of the ground provided by balloons became a vital military asset. At the very beginning of the ballooning age, the army of Revolutionary France had formed a balloon corps, which used hydrogen balloons to allow observers to spot enemy movements.

At the battle of Fleurus on 26 June 1794, General Morlot stayed aloft for ten hours, watching the maneuvers of the Austrian Army. Written messages were hauled up and down the balloon cable, so that he could direct his own forces, and the result was a decisive French victory.

In the USA, when fighting broke out between the North and the South, most balloonists signed up with the Union Army. Unfortunately, their early efforts were blighted by the stresses and strains of operating captive balloons in the field, especially when these had to be inflated from a gas main and then towed around the countryside in a fully inflated condition. John Wise constructed a special balloon for army service with an iron bottom to the gondola to keep bullets at bay.

It was also loaded with rifles, rations, ammunition, and grenades to rain down on enemy positions, but, when it was being towed across a bridge over the Potomac, it was seized by a gust of wind and torn from the hands of the balloon party. It floated away with its precious cargo toward Confederate territory, and, to prevent its cargo falling into enemy hands, they managed to shoot it down over Arlington.

Wise's colleague, John La Mountain, was more successful. He and his balloon were sent by ship to Fort Monroe in southeastern Virginia in July 1861, and, on his first ascent from the fort at the end of that month, he was able to report the presence of two Confederate encampments. A week later, he took his balloon on the armed transport *Fanny* on a sortie up the James River. He made a series of observation flights with his balloon tethered by cable to the deck of the ship, making it the world's first aircraft carrier. Later, he made other flights from the deck of the tug *Adriatic* so that these two small craft formed the world's first carrier task force.

But these observation balloons were limited in the extent of their view by their fixed positions. So La Mountain's greatest feat was to use his old *Atlantic* balloon to make free flights over enemy territory. When the wind at ground level blew from the west, he would ascend and drift over the Confederate lines to observe what the enemy was doing. When he had seen all he wanted to, he would jettison ballast from the gondola, so that the balloon rose to higher altitudes, where the airstream usually blew from the east, carrying him back to his own side.

It was an exceedingly courageous act, and he made a series of flights without being hit by Confederate fire. In all that time, the nearest he came to disaster was from a Northern unit, which did not know about his reconnaissance flights. Seeing his balloon approach from the east, they took it for a Confederate observer who had broken away from his mooring, and opened fire. He managed to land without a scratch, but within six months his career was over. Having fallen out with Thaddeus Lowe, who had the ear of the Union High Command (see box on page 34) he was forced to leave army service.

Confederate balloons

In comparison with the intrepid efforts of the balloonists on the Union side, the Southern armies had little aerial help. As the Northern army of Grant and Sherman advanced from Fort Monroe, the Confederates under General Johnston had one single observation balloon to keep the threat in view. This was not even a gas balloon, but a cotton Montgolfière, and one that did not carry its fire aloft with it. Instead it was launched above a stove burning an unpromising mixture of pine nuts which had been soaked in turpentine, so its range was severely limited.

A young captain on Johnston's staff, named John Randolph Bryan, made a series of tethered flights to keep the Union forces under observation. Once the balloon had been spotted, every appearance called up a hail of fire, so an entire team of artillery horses was kept to haul the balloon down as fast as possible.

To avoid enemy gunfire, Bryan made his last flight at night, in bright moonlight, taking off from woodland outside Yorktown, Virginia. All was going well until a soldier became entangled in the balloon cable, and Bryan and the balloon had to be cut free, to drift helplessly across the enemy lines.

Fortunately, the rapidly cooling balloon then began drifting back toward the Confederate positions. Less fortunately, the Southern sentries made the usual mistake of thinking any balloon drifting *toward* them was hostile, and opened fire on it. It drifted slowly across the York River, but managed to reach the friendly bank on the other side before finally collapsing for lack of warm air in the envelope.

Bryan's brave but doomed hot-air balloon was replaced by the much more colorful and glamorous "silk dress balloon." This was made from bolts of silk in assorted colors, all varnished with a mixture made by dissolving railway coach springs in naphtha, which led to a romantic fiction that the material had been made available by Southern women donating their silk ball gowns.

Unfortunately, it was even less successful than its predecessor. Because the Confederates had no field generators, it had to be inflated at the Richmond Gas Works, in Virginia, and towed to its launching site by lashing it to a locomotive on the York River Railroad. When the fighting moved away from the railroad route in summer 1862, the balloon was lashed to the deck of the Confederate armed steam tug *Teaser* on the James River. On 4 July 1862, the tug ran aground on a sand bar at Turkey Bend, where it was damaged by the Union ironclad *Monitor*, and the balloon was captured.

A second silk balloon followed, and this was inflated at Charleston Gas Works in West Virginia. But in July 1863 it escaped from its moorings with no one aboard, drifted across the lines and was captured by Union soldiers. By then both sides had rather lost interest in balloons: the South from their lack of success in operating them, and the North from bureaucratic inertia. Yet less than a decade later, military balloons would once again come into their own, in the Franco-Prussian War.

ABOVE: *The converted coal barge* G W Parke Custis, *used as an observation balloon carrier on the Potomac for the Northern Army during the Civil War*

Lowe and the Civil War

The most successful of all the Civil War balloonists was Thaddeus Lowe. He had a narrow escape before the fighting broke out, when flying in his 20,000-cubic-foot balloon *Enterprise* from his home town of Cincinnati in April 1861. This was meant to be a proving flight which would eventually enable him to make an Atlantic crossing. Conditions were right for a successful take-off at 3.30 in the morning of the 20th, and at first he drifted to the east, exactly as he had planned.

Unfortunately, the wind shifted, carrying Lowe and his balloon more to the southeast, over the Appalachian Mountains into South Carolina, where he came down near the town of Unionville just after midday. There he was met by a hostile crowd, and he had to keep them away with shots from his revolver. He agreed to go with them to the jail at Unionville, where he was locked up, until the owner of the local hotel recognized him and arranged for him to be released and put on the train to Columbia, where he was arrested as a Northern spy.

ABOVE RIGHT: *Although the early promise of Lowe's efforts was wasted, the US Army later became convinced of the value of observation balloons, like this one at San Juan Hill in the Spanish-American War of 1898*

BELOW: *Thaddeus Lowe used portable field generators to inflate observation balloons with hydrogen whenever they were needed, instead of having to keep them inflated for weeks on end*

For a second time he was released, but the approaching war had eliminated all hopes of making the ocean crossing.

Instead, Lowe went to Washington, where he approached President Lincoln to plead the cause of the observation balloon in the newly opened war. He was appointed official balloonist to the Army of the Potomac, and soon proved his worth. After the Union defeat at the First Battle of Bull Run, Lowe took off from Fort Corcoran in the tethered balloon *Enterprise* on 21 July 1861, and reached a height of 15,000 feet, where he was able to report that the Confederates were not following up their victory, thereby avoiding a Northern rout.

Lowe was a great innovator, and had already developed a way of sending messages down the balloon cable by electric telegraph. On 24 September, he was able to direct the Union artillery, firing on Confederate positions at Falls Church. He also developed a powerful searchlight for night-time take-offs. But his most significant achievement was the development of a cumbersome portable hydrogen generator. Twelve were made in all, mounted on horse-drawn wagons and using sulfuric acid and iron filings.

Lowe also produced the first specially designed aircraft carrier in November 1861, by having a coal barge called the *G. W. Parke Custis* fitted with a launching and landing deck, for operations on the Potomac. His tireless efforts helped avoid Union defeats at Fairoaks and Gaines' Mill, and the Confederates had to waste time and effort in concealing their encampments, and placing dummy positions to mislead the eyes in the sky.

Yet, after two years of success, a reorganization of the army command placed Thaddeus Lowe and his team under an army engineer who thought them of no military value. Lowe resigned his appointment, and his corps broke up shortly afterwards— it was a golden opportunity wasted.

Balloons and the Siege of Paris

In September 1870 the advancing Prussian forces pushed back their French adversaries and succeeded in surrounding Paris. On the 23rd a French balloonist named Jules Duruof took off from a city square with a cargo of mail, and was blown safely across the Prussian siege lines to land near Evreux, 50 miles west of the capital. Though he dropped visiting cards on the enemy troops as he flew over them, his successful flight promised an essentially one-way line of communication.

Then a Paris breeder of racing pigeons called Van Roosebeke proposed that any more balloons leaving Paris should include carrier pigeons among their loads. These could then return to the city with messages from outside, opening up a two-way dialogue. The next problem, the limited supply of balloons existing in the beleaguered city, would take more planning to solve.

The last prewar balloon to leave departed at the end of September, but by then production lines had been set up in two Parisian railway terminals, the Gare du Nord and the Gare d'Orléans. Because the trains no longer ran, as the routes had been cut by the Prussians, these were ideal buildings to hold ranks of seamstresses and rope-makers along the silent platforms. Each completed balloon was filled with air and hung from the high station roofs to check for leaks.

BELOW: *Prussian troops besieging Paris in 1871, during the Franco-Prussian War, try to bring down a dispatch-carrying balloon from the beleaguered capital*

The balloons were made from cotton cloth, as cheaply as possible, as they had to make only one flight apiece. One of them carried the French politician Léon Gambetta, who was wounded in the hand by a shot from a Prussian rifleman, but nevertheless escaped to revive French spirits. In all, 66 balloons left Paris during the siege, but the chance winds sent many on long and sometimes fatal journeys. One balloon reached Norway after a flight of almost 2,000 miles; others landed in Holland and Belgium; and another one flew all the way to Munich in the heart of Germany, where its intrepid crew was arrested and imprisoned on landing.

When an armistice was signed and the siege was raised, five balloons were ready to fly. During the course of the fighting more than 100 passengers had been carried across the German lines, in spite of specially designed anti-aircraft guns being used to try to shoot them down. The balloons also carried more than 2½ million letters and more than 400 pigeons to carry return messages. These were recorded on microfilm, so that the equivalent of 5,000 letters could be carried by a single bird, and they could be read and transcribed with the aid of a specially developed projector.

But the siege of Paris was a special case, and it was becoming increasingly clear that the military usefulness of balloons was limited, especially as new types of gun made them increasingly vulnerable to enemy fire. The next step in military lighter-than-air flight would have to wait for the invention of the airship, though civilian interest in balloons entered a new phase with the fashion for balloon racing, and the rise of the sporting balloon.

BELOW: *Prussian troops besieging Paris in 1871, during the Franco-Prussian War, try to bring down a dispatch-carrying balloon from the beleaguered capital*

Ballooning for fun

Recreational ballooning reached its peak at the turn of the century, when clubs for wealthy private balloonists sprang up all over the world. In England the Royal Aero Club was originally founded in September 1901 as an organization for private balloonists, and it maintained a field at the Hurlingham Club on the fringes of London with its own twelve-inch gas main, balloons for hire, and qualified professional balloonists for those who lacked the qualifications to pilot their own craft.

At first, sporting balloonists concentrated on establishing and breaking long-distance records. In time, though, this became more difficult and time-consuming, so that other competitive events were organised. Among the most famous were the Gordon Bennet races, sponsored by James Gordon Bennet of the *New York Herald*, who put up a trophy and an annual cash prize for competition between members of all the national balloon clubs.

The first race started from Paris on 30 September 1906, and was won by an American balloonist, Frank P. Lahm, who landed his balloon, the *United States*, at Fylingdales in northern England after a flight of 401 miles. The Gordon Bennet races were run every year until 1938, apart from the war years and aftermath 1914 to 1919, and the peak of the Great Depression in 1931. Some started from European cities such as Berlin, Zürich, and Stuttgart, and others from St Louis, Kansas City, Cleveland (Ohio), Detroit, Birmingham (Alabama), and Chicago. Only one was won by a Frenchman, and two more by Swiss balloonists. Four were won by Polish balloonists, two by Germans and no fewer than seven by Belgians. But American balloonists won ten of these races, the largest total of any single nation.

ABOVE: *A sports balloon climbs into the sky from London's Hurlingham Club*

RIGHT: *The Hurlingham gas main inflates a group of competitive balloons while the crowd looks on*

OPPOSITE PAGE: *Massed hydrogen balloons jockeying for position before a large and enthusiastic crowd at the 1904 Air Fair in Milan, Italy*

3. Into the Wind–the Airship

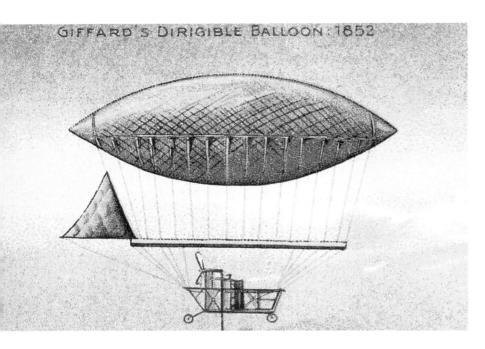

GIFFARD'S DIRIGIBLE BALLOON : 1852

ABOVE: *At last a craft which could be steered into a very light wind: Giffard's powered dirigible of 1852*

From the very beginning of ballooning, it was obvious that the potential of the balloon was severely limited by its inability to fly anywhere but with the wind. This lent it such a high degree of unpredictability that it could be useful only as a tethered observation point, a sporting plaything, or a transport where, as in the siege of Paris, the actual direction of flight was not particularly important.

Though experiments with fans, sails, paddles, and oars had continued for years, none of these expedients had ever proved to be of the slightest use. What was needed was a power unit light enough to be carried aloft, and powerful enough to push the balloon envelope and gondola, with all their considerable air resistance, into the wind quickly enough to steer a course relative to the ground. Yet that apparently simple objective was to occupy the most inventive minds in the ballooning world for years on end.

Final success was the prize of a French balloonist called Henri Giffard. He had produced a series of inventions to improve the performance of steam railroad locomotives before he became interested in ballooning. He designed a large captive balloon for the Paris International Exhibition of 1867, with a capacity of 176,500 cubic feet, which gave flights for the visiting public (see page 66).

As might be expected from such an experienced engineer, the whole project was carefully designed from the start. The balloon was operated by a powerful steam-driven winch, the cables were specially strong, and the construction of the envelope was intended to stand up to the severest loads. In all, it carried a total of 35,000 people before it was damaged in a collision with a free-flying balloon.

Giffard's next step was to bring his experience with steam engines to his new-found interest in balloons. He designed a balloon with a cigar-shaped envelope 144 feet long and 39 feet across at its widest point. This envelope was covered with a net which supported a 66-foot pole slung beneath it, parallel to the axis of the envelope. This carried a small triangular steering sail at its rear end, and in the middle was a small gondola with enough room for Giffard, a miniature steam engine which weighed only 550 pounds, and a three-bladed propeller some 10 feet in diameter.

On 24 September 1852, Giffard took off in this unusual-looking craft from the Hippodrome in Paris, in front of the usual large crowd. The spectators were astonished to see the steam engine emit a series of puffs of smoke, and the balloon could be seen moving forward on a straight course. Giffard flew steadily to the southwest and finally landed at the village of Trappe some 15 miles from the capital.

Though his speed had been little faster than walking pace, he had managed to go where he wanted to, and not where the wind was pleased to carry him. On a later flight, he demonstrated his aircraft's independence of the wind even more graphically by flying in a circle. The first airship had arrived, though two Swiss-born inventors had previously made inroads towards airship design (see box on page 40).

Giffard's initial inspiration for his first dirigible, or steerable balloon, had begun in 1850, when he had watched a Paris clockmaker, named Pierre Jullien of Villejuif, demonstrate a model airship, powered solely by a clockwork motor driving two propellers set side by side, at the same Hippodrome from which Giffard himself was to fly two years later.

LEFT: *This drawing of a highly speculative "airship" flying over New York, based on the unmistakable shape of Giffard's design, was produced to publicize a musical comedy*

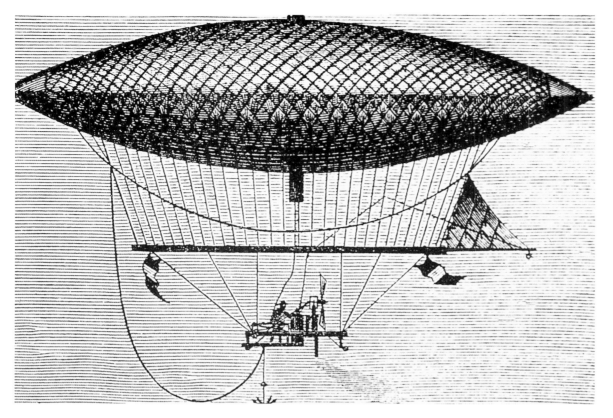

Nevertheless, what was needed to make airships viable in winds more hostile than the near-calm conditions Giffard had encountered was more power. He tried making a larger, more streamlined airship, but this became deformed in flight and, lacking any trimming device, it crashed. He then proposed a truly enormous airship, with a capacity of 7,800,000 cubic feet, which should have been capable of lifting off with a massive 30-ton steam engine, delivering enough power to guarantee a peak air speed of 45 m.p.h.

On the grounds of cost, Giffard's giant was never built. Instead, 20 years after his first airship flight, a French marine engineer named

ABOVE: *The spidery construction of Giffard's dirigible was able to support the weight of a small steam engine to provide power*

Dupuy de Lôme built an egg-shaped balloon driven by a large four-bladed propeller, geared to be driven by a crew of eight. For the first time this produced controllable forward motion, but was no faster than Giffard's steam airship. In the United States in 1878, Charles E. Ritchell built a smaller airship with a cylindrical envelope 25 feet long, which carried a framework that allowed the balloonist to turn a propeller with a set of foot pedals (see box on page 49).

Amazingly, a flight from Hartford, Connecticut, saw the airship rise and perform a circular flight in calm conditions at a speed of some 3 m.p.h. But as with its French predecessor, man-powered flight was a blind alley. Fortunately for airship development, the power plant of the future was even then waiting in the wings (see box on page 42).

The curious airship of Pauly and Egg

The story of the steerable balloon, or dirigible, nearly began 35 years before Giffard's epic flight. Two Swiss-born gunsmiths and inventors working in England, Johann Pauly and Durs Egg, produced a curious dolphin-shaped balloon, which was made from gold-beater's skin, or the outer lining of a cow's intestine, as a material that was tough, elastic, and airtight. The balloon was to be powered by oars, and it used an ingenious balancing system which consisted of a box filled with sand, which could be pulled backwards or forwards by cables, to help trim the craft. It also used an internal airbag or ballonet to help keep the envelope

filled if gas should escape, but as an airship it proved a failure, and was dubbed "Egg's Folly."

New sources of power

The first internal-combustion engines offered new ways of providing airborne power, but the original designs were disappointing. More promising was an airship built by the brothers Gaston and Albert Tissandier, which was shown in model form at the 1881 Electrical Exhibition in Paris, France. The full-size version had a 37,500-cubic-foot envelope supporting an open-framework gondola with batteries and an electric motor driving a twin-blade propeller. The balloon flew in 1883, and achieved a speed of 3 m.p.h. in still air, which seemed to be the absolute limit for airship performance.

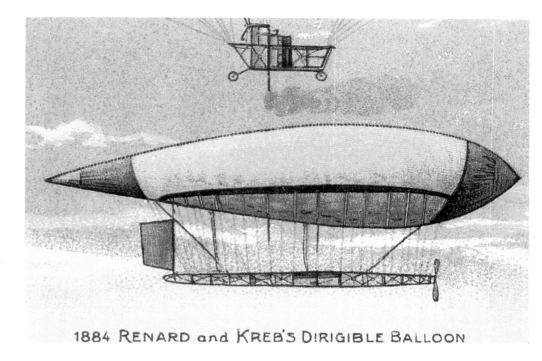

1884 RENARD and KREB'S DIRIGIBLE BALLOON

Yet the same principle was used by two French Army engineer officers, Charles Renard and Arthur Krebs, who were part financed by the former Interior Minister Léon Gambetta, who had made his escape from Paris by balloon during the Franco-Prussian War not long before. Their airship, *La France*, was almost twice the size of the Tissandiers', at 66,000 cubic feet, but it carried special lightweight batteries and an electric motor delivering more than six times as much power.

The airship was thoroughly well planned with a propeller that could be tilted to provide extra lift to cushion the shock of landing, sliding weights to keep the airship level, and air bags called ballonets inside the main envelope to improve stability. On 9 August 1884, the two engineers climbed aboard, and the airship took off from an army parade ground at Chalais-Meudon on the southwestern side of Paris. They flew south, then west, to circle over Villacoublay, before turning back northeast into the teeth of a northerly wind to arrive back over their starting point, where they landed after a flight of 23 minutes. This was the most impressive airship flight yet.

Others persevered with internal-combustion engines. In Germany, a Protestant minister from Leipzig, Dr Karl Wölfert, produced a whole series of unsuccessful and even dangerous experimental airships, using manually driven propellers. But in 1887 the inventor Gottlieb Daimler read an account of Wölfert's efforts, and suggested he might be able to make use of one of Daimler's new gasoline engines.

The result was a small balloon of 8,750 cubic feet, which was powered by a single-cylinder vertical gasoline engine of 2 horsepower, driving two propellers. It took off from outside the Daimler factory on 12 August 1888, flown by a factory mechanic who succeeded in relighting the engine with a screened candle when the hot-tube ignition failed to cope with the slipstream. Once again, though, performance could cope with little more than the calmest of conditions.

Sadly, this earlier promise was overshadowed by a series of mishaps, culminating in a disaster on a flight from Tempelhof field in Berlin in June 1897, when the ignition system set fire to escaping gas from the balloon, causing it to catch fire and plunge to the ground, killing Wölfert and his fellow crewman. The accident confirmed the French in their feeling that the internal-combustion engine was too inherently dangerous to be a serious contender for powering airships.

Five months later, another demonstration at Tempelhof ended in a crash, though the pilot of the Austrian David Schwartz's extraordinary aluminum-covered rigid airship escaped with his life. For all that,

TOP: *Rénard and Krebs' dirigible had a different shape from Giffard's, and used an electric motor driven by lightweight batteries*

ABOVE: *Gaston and Albert Tissandier's gondola was large enough to carry banks of heavy batteries to provide its power*

ABOVE: *A medallion struck to commemorate the record-breaking flight of Henri Santos-Dumont*

the interest of Germany in airship development was well and truly kindled. One of the spectators of these early flights was the Count Ferdinand von Zeppelin, who had also been attached to the Northern Army as an officer in the Prussian Army, and had seen Lowe's achievements at first hand. His name would come to symbolize the military and luxury civilian airships of the future.

Henri Santos-Dumont

In sharp contrast, the French seemed to have lost interest in airship production after *La France* and its spectacular flight. When the situation changed, it was due to an expatriate Brazilian named Henri Santos-Dumont, who was determined to produce a truly viable airship.

He was one of the first to own an automobile, in his case a little de-Dion-powered tricycle, and he was convinced this type of power unit would drive an airship even through contrary breezes.

Made for the job— the internal-combustion engine

Finding a suitable source of power to drive a dirigible was a difficult technological problem, since weight was so severely limited. Steam power, clockwork, and electricity were all very well for powering experimental airships for short distances at low speeds, but lacked the necessary power-to-weight ratio to provide the performance needed for a practical long-distance dirigible.

The only genuine solution was the internal-combustion engine, itself a creation of the later part of the nineteenth century. While Karl Benz and Gottlieb Daimler were taking the first hesitant steps toward developing the automobile, others were able to harness their power units to quite different purposes. Dr Karl Wölfert, a Leipzig bookseller and clergyman, was also an inventor. When an article on the test flight of his experimental dirigible appeared in a Leipzig newspaper in 1887, Gottlieb Daimler invited Wölfert to visit him at Cannstatt, near Stuttgart, with a view to collaborating on developing a powered airship.

The result was a small, single-cylinder Daimler engine delivering 4 horsepower, with an ingenious transmission system. This allowed the engine to drive an airscrew on a horizontal shaft to propel the airship forwards, and another airscrew on a vertical shaft to provide additional lift. The dirigible, fitted with this engine and transmission, made a successful flight of 2.5 miles from the grounds of Daimler's motor works at Seelberg to nearby Kornwestheim, in still-air conditions on 12 August 1888.

Unfortunately, this success spurred Wölfert to attempt much more. He built a much larger dirigible with a 28,000-cubic-foot envelope, with a more powerful engine, which was completed in 1897. On the evening of 14 June, he took off to demonstrate it to a large crowd at Tempelhof in Berlin. When he started the engine, exhaust flames emerged perilously close to the envelope filled with hydrogen. He applied power, and Wölfert and his engineer ascended to a height of 3,000 feet, when the craft caught fire and exploded, killing both of them.

Ein 4 PS Daimler-Motor, 1888 erstmalig als Luftschiffmotor verwendet
(In der Gondel der Leipziger Buchhändler Dr. Wölfert.)

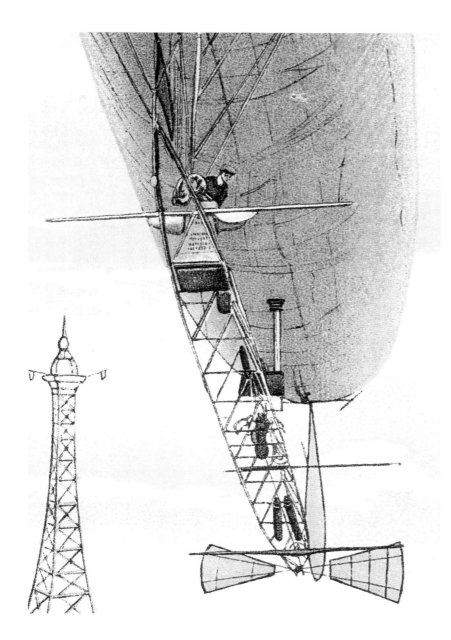

Yet Santos-Dumont's first dirigibles were no more successful than those of his rivals. His first airship took off from the Paris Zoological Gardens and ended up in a tree. His second lacked stability for the want of a rigid keel, but by then he was dedicated to spending the Santos-Dumont family coffee fortune on the making of dirigibles.

He set up an assembly line in a large shed on a field at St-Cloud, just outside the city, which he rented from the French Aero Club. He had gas mains connected and set up his own hydrogen-generating system.

This was to be the scene of his most spectacular exploit. In 1900 a wealthy French oil producer, Henri Deutsch de la Meurthe, had put up a prize of 100,000 francs for the first person to take off from St-Cloud, fly round the Eiffel Tower, and return, all within half an hour. This was equivalent to an average speed of over 15 m.p.h. and was a daunting challenge.

Nevertheless, Santos-Dumont was determined to meet it. He tried with the fifth of his airships, but failed. He then tried again with an improved number 6, which apart from its gasoline engine was still very similar to *La France*, and took off from St-Cloud on the afternoon of 19 October 1901. Fortunately the wind was with him on the outbound journey, and he sailed round the top of the Eiffel Tower only nine minutes after take-off, thanks to a helpful tailwind.

On the return journey, though, the wind was against him, and, as if this were not enough, his engine started to misfire. At one point Santos-Dumont had to take his hands off the controls to coax some life into the engine, and risked being blown off course and losing ground as a result. But his luck held, and he arrived back over St-Cloud with less than half a minute to spare.

The prize was his, and with it the fame that he truly coveted. He gave half the cash prize to the poor people of Paris and the rest to the workers at his airship factory at St-Cloud. But his real reputation rested with his spectacular proof that the gasoline-powered airship had a future after all, and with his trips around the city using his smaller airships almost as airborne cars (see box below).

The rise and fall of the Zeppelins

Though airships continued to be built in France after Santos-Dumont switched his interest to airplanes from 1905, other countries were starting to experiment with varying degrees of success. In spite of the pioneering work of the Civil War balloonists, the first American airship did not appear until 1908 when Thomas Scott Baldwin, an experienced balloonist and parachute jumper, produced a cylindrical envelope with tapered ends which carried a long framework below it with a rudder at one end and an engine-driven propeller at the other.

BELOW: *The first true non-rigid airship made by the Lebaudy brothers for the French Army, nicknamed* Le Jaune *because of the bright yellow color of its envelope, went on show at the 1903 Paris Exposition*

Santos-Dumont—the Magnificent Man in his Flying Machine

Henri Santos-Dumont tended to work through trial and error, rather than from truly original and inspired designs. Often his airships were unstable in pitch, and tended to climb or descend unpredictably. He avoided this by flying low and using a trail rope, just like his balloonist predecessors, and his greatest achievement was in showing just how practical a form of transport an airship could be, in the almost empty skies of the time. After his 21,965-cubic-foot airship number 6 had won the Deutsch award, he then built number 9, a much smaller egg-shaped dirigible of just over one-third the capacity.

This proved controllable enough for him to wander the streets and boulevards of Paris at just over treetop height. To the Parisians, the small and dapper Brazilian became a familiar sight, sailing over the capital on his way from his workshops at Neuilly St-James to his favorite city-center restaurant, "La Cascade." As he dined out with his friends, his airship floated outside the establishment, tethered by a long mooring rope. On one occasion, he called at his home on the corner of the Champs Elysées and the Rue Washington, for a morning coffee, leaving the airship outside the front door.

This was the *US Military I*, and it was assigned to the US Army Signal Corps. Its envelope was made of two layers of Japanese silk with a central layer of vulcanized rubber and it carried an elaborate biplane elevator for controlling its pitch attitude. It made a number of flights from Fort Omaha in Nebraska and from Fort Meyers in Virginia, but led to no further experiments for the best part of 20 years.

In the meantime the focus of airship development shifted to Germany, and in particular to Count Zeppelin. He had decided as early as 1874 that the airships of the future would have to be as large as possible, to create the maximum lift. They would need to use part of this lift to carry powerful engines, to give them speed and

endurance, and independence from the weather. They must also have a large rigid frameworks, with lifting gas contained in gas cells rather than in single envelopes.

Beyond this, Zeppelin's thinking was limited by his lack of engineering experience. Fortunately, his ideas were lucid enough to direct those with the right knowledge, and, when he was forced to retire as a general in the German Army after having offended the Kaiser in 1890, he was able to devote his time to building larger and more powerful airships.

It took him six years to raise enough capital to found the Zeppelin Airship Company, and another three years before construction work on the first Zeppelin airship could begin, in 1899. His original inspiration had been translated into a framework made up of circular cross-frames linked by longitudinal beams, or stringers, for strength and lightness. Seventeen separate gas cells were shaped to fit the space enclosed by the framework, and these were filled with hydrogen.

Cars for engines, crew, and passengers were slung below the main structure, which was covered with a sort of varnished linen, like the early airplanes. The bottom of the hull was reinforced by a long keel, and a sliding weight could be controlled from the cars to make the airship climb or descend. The whole structure was assembled in a huge hangar, suspended on floats on the surface of Lake Constance, on the border between Germany and Switzerland.

Zeppelin LZ1, as the new airship was identified, took to the air for the first time from a floating raft on the lake in the fall of 1900, but it soon became clear that performance and strength were disappointing. The future looked bleak for Zeppelin, with the money running out, and LZ1 was broken up in 1901. Yet the Count succeeded in raising funds for another airship by running a lottery and appeals in newspapers.

LZ2 was completed in November 1905, but wrecked in bad weather on its second flight in January of the following year. LZ3 flew in October 1906, and was put into service by the German Army, who saw all too well the value of an airborne weapons platform.

But Zeppelin's problems were far from over. LZ4 was sent on a much publicized long-distance flight to reassure the army that airships could stand up to tough service conditions. After flying for 20 hours, the airship was returning to base when it had to land for engine repairs at Stuttgart. However, a sudden gust pushed the airship into power cables, and it caught fire and exploded.

By now, however, Zeppelin was a public hero, and that same public rushed to subscribe to a fund to keep German airship development alive. In all, 6 million Reichsmarks flowed into the Zeppelin coffers, to be turned over to a trust fund for the Zeppelin Airship Company. As a result there emerged from the works a whole succession of progressively larger, more powerful, and more reliable airships, capable of carrying heavier loads over longer distances.

For example, the LZ6 of 1909 was taken over by the new German Airship Travel Company but was destroyed by accident after a year in service. Its successor, LZ7, was officially named *Deutschland* and carried 32 passengers on a demonstration flight, but engine breakdown and stormy weather brought it down in the Teutoburger Forest, without any injuries. Not until LZ10, which carried the name *Schwaben*, did the airship begin to fulfill its real potential. In less than a year, from its first flight on 15 July 1911 to its loss by fire on 28 June 1912, once again without any casualties, the airship carried a total of 1,553 passengers on 218 different long-distance flights.

By 1912 Zeppelins were making

TOP: *By the time Zeppelin had built the LZ4, his airships were capable of making long-distance endurance trips to impress the German Army, but were still fatally vulnerable to bad weather*

ABOVE: *Zeppelin LZ10 made more than 200 long distance flights and carried more than 1500 passengers*

OPPOSITE PAGE: *Balloons at war again: a Royal Navy "P" class minesweeper sets off a drifting mine which has been spotted by the observer in the kite balloon towed behind the ship*

international flights, to Denmark and Sweden. But this promising development was halted by the outbreak of World War I in August 1914, when airships were turned to grimmer purposes altogether (see box on page 55). Even when hostilities were over, many of the surviving Zeppelins were wrecked by their crews, as the German High Seas Fleet was scuttled at Scapa Flow in the Orkneys after surrendering to the British. The survivors were seen as weapons of war, every bit as much as captured tanks and submarines, and many were handed over to the Allies as reparations.

ABOVE: *Eyes of the Fleet: naval users wanted airships like this British rigid dirigible flying over Royal Navy warships, as an answer to the eternal problem of tracking the enemy*

OPPOSITE TOP RIGHT: *The complex and spidery framework of the LZ126 takes shape at Friedrichshafen—when finished, the airship joined the US Navy as the USS Los Angeles*

LZ126—*Los Angeles*

Two of these were to be handed over to the USA, but negotiations eventually produced a different and more advantageous deal. Instead of taking over the wartime Zeppelins, the United States would take delivery of a new purpose-built Zeppelin, the LZ126, for service with the US Navy. This would preserve the Zeppelin company as a going concern, and, because postwar restrictions limited German aircraft production, they would have to form a partnership with the Goodyear Tire and Rubber Company, to give the fledgling American airship industry a flying start.

LZ126 first flew at Friedrichshafen on 27 August 1924. After three more test flights, the airship set out across the Atlantic on 12 October, reaching its destination of Lakehurst, New Jersey, three days later, after a flight of 4,660 miles which lasted more than 80 hours. There the airship was grounded, to have the gasbags refilled with the much safer, nonflammable helium. Unfortunately, this was so rare and expensive that the operation could be carried out only by grounding the first US-produced postwar airship, the USS *Shenandoah* (see box on page 51), and transferring helium between the two airships.

LZ126 was renamed ZR3 *Los Angeles*, and proved very successful. Over eight months she made a series of flights as far afield as Bermuda, before returning to allow the helium to be transferred back to the *Shenandoah*. Unfortunately, the loss of the *Shenandoah* in stormy weather in September 1925 meant new supplies of helium had to be produced, though, when *Los Angeles* flew again, it started three years of service which opened up a whole range of new possibilities.

It repeated, in airship terms, the operations of Lowe and his converted barge in the Civil War. In this case, the *Los Angeles* was moored to a special mast fitted to the deck of the tender *Patoka*. It also succeeded in landing on the huge flight deck of the US Navy aircraft carrier *Saratoga*. But its most startling achievement was acting as an aircraft carrier in its own right.

The first American airships

Professor C. E. Ritchell of Hartford, Connecticut, produced a small cylindrical airship in 1878, in which the pilot rode astride a bicycle seat slung below the envelope. By pedaling furiously, he was able to drive a four-bladed airscrew on the end of a long framework, to power and steer the craft. On 12 June 1878, it made its one and only recorded flight, rising to almost 200 feet and staying aloft for more than an hour, but never played a real part in airship development.

The first practical American airship was built by Thomas Scott Baldwin in 1904. He called the 52-foot dirigible the *California Arrow*, and fitted it with a two-cylinder, 5-horsepower engine made by the aviation pioneer Glenn H. Curtiss. Flown by pilot Roy Knabenshue, the airship made its first public flight at the premier international flying machine competition, held at the 1904 International Exhibition at St Louis in Missouri, USA.

By 1907, the city was organizing airship races, and other inventors were busy building designs of their own. The youngest must have been Cromwell Dixon from Seattle in Washington, who was aged just 14 when he produced a small pedal-powered airship called *Moon*, which

was later fitted with an engine. The cylindrical envelope was sewn together by his mother, who was rewarded by being allowed to fly the airship for herself on at least one occasion.

Baldwin went on to imitate his predecessor Henri Santos-Dumont in building a whole series of airships. In 1908 he produced a 20,000-cubic-foot cylindrical dirigible 95 feet long. It was powered by a 20-horsepower Curtiss engine, and its large

rectangular rudder was painted with a huge Stars and Stripes.

Baldwin entered it for a US government competition, with a prize of $10,000 for the producer of a practical military machine which could be steered and controlled to follow a set course. Baldwin demonstrated his airship at Fort Myers on 18 August 1908, and the US Army was so impressed that the prize was awarded immediately and the airship was bought by the Signal Corps.

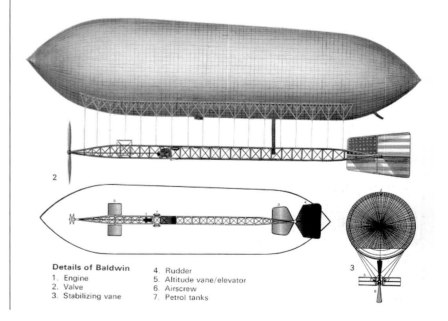

Details of Baldwin
1. Engine
2. Valve
3. Stabilizing vane
4. Rudder
5. Altitude vane/elevator
6. Airscrew
7. Petrol tanks

ABOVE: *The USS Shenandoah with two Curtiss biplane fighters approaching the trapeze gear (just ahead of the leading engines) from behind and below*

RIGHT: *A fighter from the USS Macon (see box on page 52) hooks on to the trapeze gear*

The airship flew at its maximum speed of around 80 m.p.h., while a naval biplane fighter approached it from underneath at a similar speed. This allowed the pilot to maneuver to engage a trapeze hanging below the hull of the airship with a hook mounted on the airplane's upper wing. Once hooked on, fighter and crew could be hoisted into a hangar space inside the airship, to be launched again later.

Unusually for a hard-working military airship, the *Los Angeles* lived on into old age. With public funds short in the Depression years, the airship was laid up in 1932. She never flew again, and was finally broken up in early 1940, with the approach of a new world war.

The USS *Shenandoah*

The US Navy's first rigid airship was based on the design of a Zeppelin captured in 1917, with an internal aluminum framework. Individual sections were made at the Naval Aircraft Factory in Philadelphia, and these were assembled in a huge hangar at the Naval Air Station at Lakehurst, New Jersey. The *Shenandoah*, with an official number ZR-1, made its maiden flight on 4 September 1923 filled with helium, so that its lifting capacity was less than predicted when originally designed for hydrogen, since helium was then in short supply.

The design included a specially strengthened nose section allowing it to be left moored to a special mast, and trials were carried out at sea with a special mooring tender, the USS *Patoka*, which had been fitted with a mooring mast. But in service the airship proved vulnerable to bad weather, on one occasion being ripped away from its Lakehurst mooring by the fury of a January gale. With some of the crew on board at the time, they were able to start the engines and ride out the storm until it was safe to return to base.

On the night of 3 September 1925, after two years in service, the *Shenandoah* was hit by a storm while flying over Ohio. An upcurrent carried the airship to an altitude where the helium-filled gasbags started to burst under the excess pressure. The valves that would normally have relieved this pressure were closed to save the rare and expensive helium, and the stresses of the storm broke the airship into three parts. The nose section with seven aboard, and the rear section with 22 crew members, made safe landings, but the center section with the remaining 14 men was a total loss.

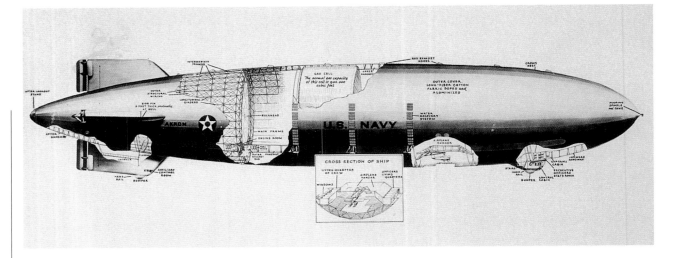

Following the loss of the USS *Shenandoah*, the US government decided the next two navy airships would be built by private enterprise, and the contract was awarded to Goodyear in Akron, Ohio. The first was the USS *Akron* (above), which flew for the first time on 23 September 1931. The design included eight engines within the hull, connected to outboard propellers which could be swung upward, downward, and backward for trimming the ship or reversing during landing maneuvers. It was designed as a fleet spotter, and was fitted with an internal hangar and a trapeze mechanism to store, launch, and retrieve up to five navy Curtiss F9C

Sparrowhawk scout planes in flight.

The airship proved highly useful in fleet exercises, but once again was vulnerable to bad weather. On a flight from Lakehurst on 3 April 1933 it had to circle far out above the ocean to avoid thunderstorms, but, when it was approaching the coast, a violent downdraft forced the *Akron* down into the sea, where it quickly broke up. Though a German tanker came to help, all but three of the crew drowned for lack of any kind of lifejackets to keep them afloat in the cold, stormy waters.

By this time the second airship, the USS *Macon* (below), was already complete. A year after the loss of her

sister, the ship was forced to return to Opalocker, Florida for temporary repairs to her internal framework, damaged by sharp evasive action during fleet exercises. She then returned to the west coast for end-of-year Pacific Fleet exercises.

Sadly, when on yet another series of exercises off California in February 1935, the temporary repairs gave way and the tail section, with its essential control surfaces, was lost. The airship settled onto the water surface, and all of the crew except two were rescued. But the entire US Navy rigid airship program sank with the *Macon*, and after her loss the USS *Los Angeles* was scrapped.

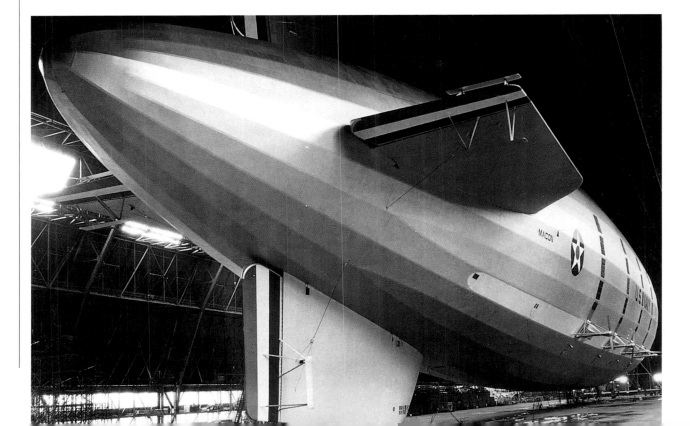

The super-Zeppelins

During the years of the *Los Angeles* proving flights, the German airship industry had recovered and surpassed its prewar efforts. With the signing of the Locarno Treaty involving Germany, France, and Belgium at the end of May 1921, restrictions on airship building had been lifted, and Dr Hugo Eckener, head of the Zeppelin works since the Count's death in 1917, decided to build a new super-Zeppelin to re-establish the supremacy of the airship for luxury long-distance travel. Once again, cash was in short supply but the ever-supportive German public put its hands in its collective pocket and delivered the financial backing necessary to make the project possible.

The result was LZ127, named *Graf Zeppelin* on 8 July 1928 in honor of the Count, on the 90th anniversary of his birth. Seventeen containers of hydrogen, held within a spidery Duralumin framework, provided enough lift to carry a load of 58 tons. Five engines were supplied from 17 fuel tanks in the bottom of the hull, and provided enough power for a top speed of 68 m.p.h. over a range of more than 6,000 miles.

These figures were impressive enough, but the keynote of the service the *Graf Zeppelin* would provide for its passengers was the kind of luxury on a scale never

TOP LEFT: *Control position of LZ127* Graf Zeppelin

ABOVE: *Luxury in flight—the* Graf Zeppelin's *dining room*

BELOW: *The LZ130, also to be named* Graf Zeppelin, *was to be an even larger replacement, but she was put into storage after the* Hindenburg *disaster (see box on page 63)*

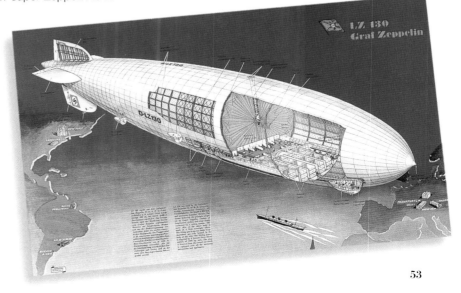

RIGHT: *The Graf Zeppelin attracts admiring crowds on a visit to England*

BELOW: *Loading the lightweight grand piano on board for the transatlantic flight*

BELOW RIGHT: *The passenger deck of the Graf Zeppelin at ground level, to allow passengers to board by retractable staircase*

seen before in airship transport. Apart from necessities like a control gondola, a navigation cabin, and a radio room, there was a curtained and carpeted lounge with armchairs and even a lightweight grand piano. There were five twin-berth sleeping cabins, with toilets and washrooms, and an electric galley and spacious dining saloon. This was space and comfort on a scale that only luxury liners could match, and with performance not far short of contemporary airliners.

The *Graf Zeppelin* flew for the first time on 18 September 1928. Two weeks later it departed for a 35-hour aerial tour of Germany. In the following 15 months, the airship would complete 50 long-distance flights, including a return crossing of the Atlantic with 20 passengers, and a Mediterranean cruise carrying 29 passengers, all carried in the utmost comfort.

The Zeppelin menace

The Zeppelins operated by the army and navy of Imperial Germany went into action on the outbreak of World War I, raiding up and down the east coast of England and targets behind the lines in France. Though numbers and bomb loads were small compared with those carried by the bomber squadrons of World War II, the airships still caused damage and casualties. Two inhabitants of the port of Great Yarmouth in England were killed by Zeppelin bombs on the night of 19 January 1915, the first civilians to die in an air raid.

At first, weather was the main danger to the airships. Later, defending fighters were able to spot the huge bulk of the airships in moonlit skies, and found them easy targets for incendiary bullets, which ignited the hydrogen in the gasbags and set them on fire. Others were brought down by anti-aircraft guns. Later designs were produced with performance that allowed them to fly higher than the defending fighters and approach their targets by a roundabout route. But the size and vulnerability of the Zeppelins made them a limited wartime weapon.

RIGHT: *Later, their hydrogen gasbags made them fatally vulnerable to incendiary bombs and bullets from enemy aircraft —Lt Warneford of the Royal Naval Air Service, destroys London-bound Zeppelin LZ37 near Brussels on 6 June, 1915 by dropping incendiary bombs on to the envelope*

It also began a round-the-world voyage on 1 August 1929 by landing at Lakehurst to pick up the American newspaper tycoon William Randolph Hearst, who had partly sponsored the trip. The airship then flew back to its home base at Lake Constance before crossing Russia non-stop to Tokyo, then across the Pacific to Los Angeles, across the USA to Lakehurst, and then finally back to Germany.

In 1930 the *Graf Zeppelin* flew to Spain and South America, to inaugurate a regular service on this route, and then flew to the Arctic, the Mediterranean, and back to the Arctic again. By 1933, this means of traveling was so reliable and well accepted that the airship was able to follow a regular timetable of long-distance flights, many of them across the Atlantic to North or South America. By 1937, this most successful of all airships had flown a total of more than a million miles and carried a total of more than 16,000 paying passengers.

What finally brought the *Graf Zeppelin* and the world she represented back to earth was the fate of her successor, the LZ129 *Hindenburg*. The original intention had been to build a design numbered LZ128 which would rely, as earlier Zeppelins had done, on the flammable hydrogen gas to provide the lift. But after the loss of the British R101 and the heavy death toll following its crash in Northern France in 1930 (see box on page 65) it was decided to produce a new design, the LZ129, which would make use of the much safer but slightly less buoyant helium, to be obtained from the United States.

Generating enough lift with helium meant a larger structure, and the *Hindenburg* was designed in 1931 to have almost twice the gas capacity of her stablemate. This time there would be two passenger decks, with amenities such as a writing room, promenade decks with large observation windows, and 25 single and double cabins. There was even a smoking room, with the strictest safety precautions. It was lined with

TOP LEFT: *A film captures a shot of LZ129 Hindenburg on one of her trials*

CENTER LEFT: *Memorabilia of the great airship— a Zeppelin passenger ticket*

LEFT: *Zeppelin luggage label for a lady passenger en route to Rio de Janeiro*

TOP RIGHT: *Poster advertising the two-day service by airship between Europe and New York, faster than any surface ship*

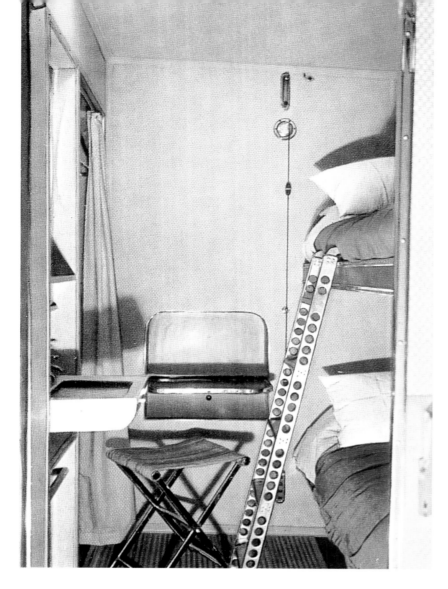

ABOVE LEFT: *A double sleeping cabin on the Hindenburg with folding stool and drilled ladder frame, designed to save weight*

ABOVE RIGHT: *The bar of the Hindenburg with murals of the Montgolfier and Charles balloons which made it all possible*

RIGHT: *Promenade deck with picture windows and the spacious dining saloon of the Hindenburg*

Crossing the Atlantic

In 1910, the American journalist Walter Wellmann set out in his 341,400-cubic-foot airship, the *America*, to cross the Atlantic. Sponsored by the *Chicago Record-Herald*, the *New York Times*, and the London *Daily Telegraph*, the airship had a steel gondola and two 80-horsepower engines driving two pairs of propellers mounted on outriggers, and capable of running on either gasoline or hydrogen piped from the airship's envelope.

The expedition was using a trail rope to maintain a constant height, which also towed tanks of spare gasoline and blocks of wood, for extra buoyancy. Underneath the airship's keel was a lifeboat, which was a vital safety precaution for crossing the ocean, but which helped overload the airship beyond its intended weight.

When the expedition took off from Atlantic City on 15 October 1910, it ran into adverse winds, the engines overheated, and time was wasted trying to unload a stowaway cat, which one of the six-man crew had smuggled aboard, into a motor launch which met the airship at sea. Finally, after three days, loss of power and lift forced the crew to abandon the airship and take to the lifeboat, where, fortunately, they were rescued the next morning by the British steamer *Trent*.

The first successful ocean crossing was eventually made by the British airship R34 in July 1919. Based on the design of wartime German Zeppelins that had been forced down over England and France, the R33 and R34 originally belonged to the Royal Navy, but were taken over by the Air Ministry. Once again there was a stowaway, in this case a human member of the crew who had officially been left behind to allow more fuel to be carried.

All went well until the airship met bad weather some 300 miles east of Newfoundland. Leaks in the engine cooling system had been plugged with chewing gum, and, after considering a refueling stop in Montreal, the pilots decided to make for Boston, and the ground handling crew were sent off to meet the ship there instead. Then conditions improved, and the destination was switched back to New York's Roosevelt Field. With no trained ground crew waiting, one of the pilots had to make a parachute jump to organize a team on the ground, and the R34 finally moored after a flight of just over 108 hours from East Fortune in Scotland.

RIGHT: *British airships R34 (the first to cross the Atlantic) and R29 in their hangar at East Fortune in Scotland*

The *Hindenburg*–Sailing through the Skies

Space, style, and comfort: two decks of passenger accommodation on LZ129 Hindenburg were made possible by the US Government's decision to ban supplies of helium following the Nazi takeover in Germany. Switching to hydrogen created more lift, and so an extra deck was added, with more sleeping cabins. They were linked by two staircases, and B deck featured, in addition to the famous smoking room, the first shower to be fitted on board an airship.

B Deck

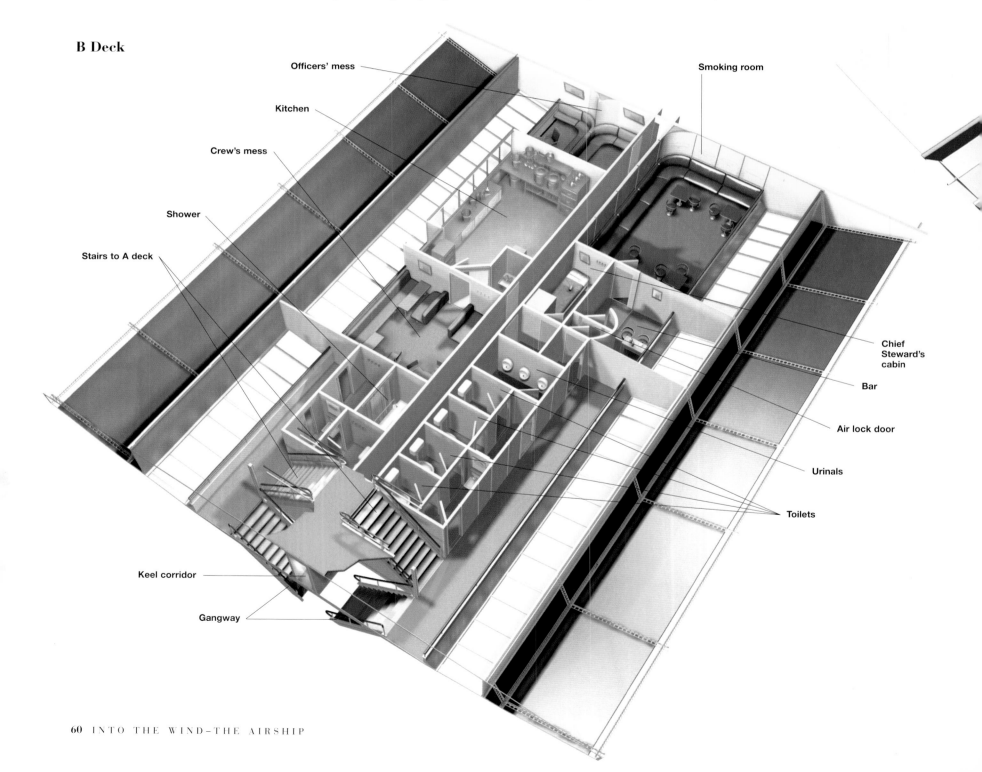

- Officers' mess
- Kitchen
- Crew's mess
- Shower
- Stairs to A deck
- Smoking room
- Chief Steward's cabin
- Bar
- Air lock door
- Urinals
- Toilets
- Keel corridor
- Gangway

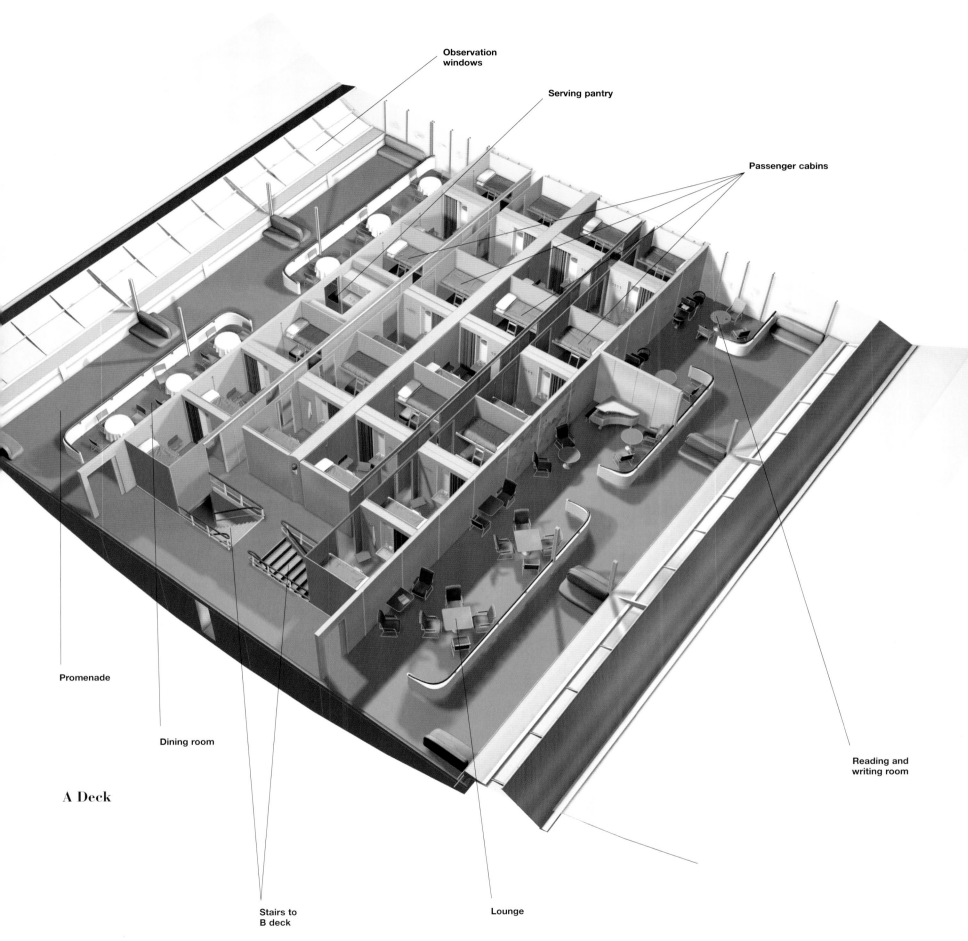

Observation windows

Serving pantry

Passenger cabins

Promenade

Dining room

Reading and writing room

A Deck

Stairs to B deck

Lounge

ABOVE: *Graphic evidence of Germany's new masters on the control surfaces of* Hindenburg

nonflammable material, sealed with an airtight door, and it was provided with the only cigarette lighter allowed on board the craft.

By the time the mighty airship, weighing more than 200 tons in take-off trim, had been completed, the world had changed. Three years before its first flight in March 1936, Adolf Hitler and his Nazi Party had come to power in Germany. The new airship would carry the swastika badge on its control surfaces as a permanent reminder of who was in control, and the United States refused to supply the expensive and strategically important helium. Instead, the Zeppelin company had to revert to hydrogen, which had proved safe enough in the *Graf Zeppelin*. One bonus was the large increase in lift, which was enough to allow nine extra cabins to be added to the passenger space.

During 1936, the new airship's career began happily enough, with 10 two-way crossings of the Atlantic to the United States and another seven to Brazil. In March 1937, the *Hindenburg* made a return flight to Rio de Janeiro and, after a major overhaul, set out for Lakehurst on 4 May, on its first scheduled North Atlantic crossing for the year. Two days later the mighty airship crossed over New York city and arrived at its mooring base at Lakehurst.

But, within minutes of its mooring, fire broke out and in less than a minute the huge airship was totally consumed (see box on page 63). With her went the lives of nearly half her crew and passengers, and the world's hopes for airship travel. The trusty *Graf Zeppelin* and her even larger successor, LZ130 *Graf Zeppelin II*, were grounded and put into storage. Three years later they were broken up, and plans for two projected United States passenger-carrying airships were canceled on the drawing board.

Why did the *Hindenburg* catch fire?

German airships, in spite of the fire risk of using hydrogen, had an outstanding safety record. Before the *Hindenburg* tragedy, no fare-paying passenger had ever been killed in an airship accident. Afterwards, there were persistent rumors of sabotage. However, both the American inquiry and a Gestapo investigation found no evidence, and it was assumed that gas had escaped inside the airship, from a sticking valve or a tank gashed by a bracing wire snapping under stress.

In this case, a single spark from static electricity in the atmosphere, or discharging through the mooring ropes, would have been enough. However, fragments of the *Hindenburg*'s skin fabric, recently analyzed at the Kennedy Space Center, were found to contain a highly flammable mix of materials,

including aluminum powder now used to propel solid-fuel rocket boosters. The American space scientist Addison Bain is convinced this was the fire source, as hydrogen produces none of the spectacular flames that consumed the airship.

Whatever the cause, her design certainly made things worse.

Intended originally to be filled with helium, the *Hindenburg* had internal ventilation shafts for releasing hydrogen which would have been used for trimming the airship. These were not needed, but, when the fire started, they acted as forced-draught chimneys and helped the blaze take hold and flourish.

Deutsche Zeppelin-Reederei

Luftschiff Hindenburg

An Bord

TOP RIGHT: *Writing paper and* (bottom left) *a menu—memorabilia from the* Hindenburg

BOTTOM RIGHT: *The blazing wreck of the* Hindenburg *falls to earth behind the Lakehurst mooring mast*

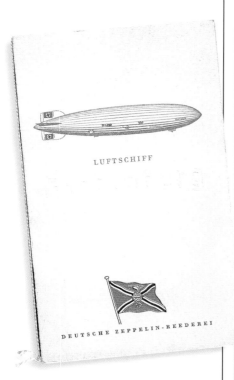

LUFTSCHIFF

DEUTSCHE ZEPPELIN-REEDEREI

TOP LEFT: *A 1936 Zeppelin timetable*

ABOVE: *This American family flew in their light aircraft to Lakehurst where they, and their airplane, were loaded on board a Zeppelin to travel to Europe*

TOP RIGHT: *Zeppelin being handled on the ground by a US Navy crew at Lakehurst*

ABOVE: *Wealthy passengers boarding the Hindenburg by its retractable ladder*

Triumph and disaster— the R38, R100, and R101

In August 1921, the British airship R38 was being transferred to the US Navy when, on the 24th, during a test flight over eastern England, the airship broke apart and crashed into the sea, killing 38 British crew and 16 US Navy men. As a result, the Royal Air Force airship organization was closed down, and future British airship efforts were limited to large airships for long-distance passenger services. These were the R100, built by private enterprise, and the R101 built by the government.

The R100 was the simpler design and in the summer of 1930 it spent almost three weeks on a double Atlantic crossing and a tour of eastern Canada and the northeastern USA. The following year its more complicated sister, the R101, was ready for its inaugural flight in the opposite direction, across Europe and the Middle East to India. Unfortunately, the preparations were rushed, the airship had engine problems and gas leaks from the envelope, and, when crossing northern France in October 1931 in increasingly bad weather, the R101 became difficult to control.

On the morning of Sunday, 5 October, the airship struck the ground on a low ridge near Bayonne and broke apart before bursting into flames. In all, 48 of the 54 passengers and crew aboard, including government ministers and high-ranking officers, died in the disaster. All British airship work was stopped, and all other surviving British airships were scrapped.

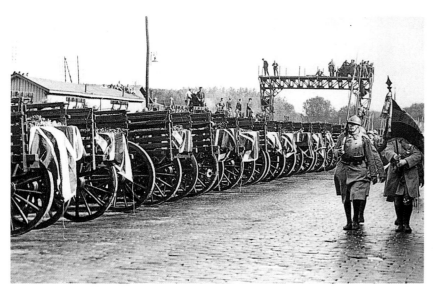

4. Balloons to the Rescue

ABOVE: *Henri Giffard's massive captive balloon introduced 35,000 people to the joys of flying at the 1867 Paris World's Fair*

As balloons and airships became more reliable, and flying became more predictable, people began to see them as useful for every kind of scientific and military purpose. But the first balloon to be developed for a sound scientific reason was fated to be the star of a tragedy, and an enduring mystery which would not be solved until more than 30 years had passed.

The story began at the Philadelphia International Exhibition of 1876, and a meeting between the American balloonist John Wise and Salomon August Andrée, a 22-year-old Swede. Andrée had been a passenger in Henri Giffard's captive balloon at the Paris World's Fair nine years before, and he had become obsessed by the prospect of developing a controllable balloon that could be used for exploring the remoter parts of the world. The idea of being able to steer the balloon to a limited extent was based on an idea by the English balloonist Charles Green, based on using a trail rope to slow the balloon down relative to the wind.

Once the balloon could be made to move *through* the air currents, instead of riding with them at their own speed, a whole new set of possibilities might open up. In theory, a set of sails could be used to allow the course of the balloon to be changed to a limited extent, using the deliberately created airflow over the balloon's envelope. While it could still only drift with the wind, its track could be angled to left or right of the line it would follow without these controls being used, when it would simply drift downwind.

In areas where the winds were known and predictable, this meant a much more useful future for balloons as part of exploration expeditions. So Andrée made use of this system on a series of trial flights in a 37,000-cubic-foot balloon called *Svea*, which seemed to bear out his claims. As a result, he was able to raise money through subscriptions to build a much larger, 151,800-cubic-foot, balloon called *Ornen* (or *Eagle*), which would be used to explore the barren Arctic from the air.

The envelope was made from three layers of Chinese silk, and there was no release valve at the top of the balloon, in case this should become blocked by snow or ice. Instead, two release valves were fitted to allow gas to escape from lower down on the balloon's envelope. The top part of the skin was varnished to prevent snow and frost sticking to it, and the balloon basket was covered for protection from the elements, and fitted with three trail ropes and eight additional ballast ropes, three sledges, and a folding lifeboat.

Andrée and his two companions, the physicist Nils Strindberg and an engineer named Knut Fraenkel, traveled on the transport ship *Virgo* in June 1896 with their equipment to Danish Isle, on the northwestern tip of the lonely Norwegian island of Spitzbergen, far to the east of Greenland. There the balloon was inflated and stored in a specially built hangar, to wait for a favorable southwesterly wind. After weeks of waiting, the window of opportunity was closing again, so the balloon was deflated and stored, and the expedition returned home, planning to try again the following year with an enlarged version.

Journey into oblivion

Finally, on 11 July 1897, the three men took off in their balloon. Unfortunately, though the wind was favorable at last, two things went wrong. When skimming away across the waves to the north-northeast, the balloon dipped and touched the sea, so the crew were forced to dump more than 450 pounds of their irreplaceable ballast to force it to climb. No sooner had their backup team seen disaster so narrowly avoided, than they found most of the all-important ballast ropes had not been tied to the balloon, and had been left lying on the seashore.

The balloon and its three occupants vanished from the face of the earth. Four days after their departure, a Norwegian sealboat shot a bird which proved to be a carrier pigeon with a message from Andrée, reporting all was well. Two years later another message was retrieved, and, a year after that, another. But the balloon and its crew were never seen alive again.

Their final fate was not revealed until more than 33 years after their disappearance. On 6 August 1930, the *Braatvag*, a modified Norwegian sealer on a scientific expedition, landed on White Island, some 250 miles to the *east* of their starting point. There they found the bodies of the explorers, amid the remains of a small camp on ground normally covered by ice and snow. When the news reached Sweden, the Swedish *Daily News* and the Danish newspaper *Politiken* chartered a ship called the *Isbjorn* (*Polar Bear*) which brought the remains back to their homeland.

Journals and photographs found with the bodies told the tragic tale of the expedition. The loss of the ballast ropes had indeed proved fatal because, without the extra weight they provided, the balloon rose so high that precious gas escaped through the safety valve to prevent the balloon from bursting. This loss of gas left them with inadequate lift when later they flew through fog and freezing rain, which settled on the outside of the envelope, and increased the balloon's weight, to the point where it came down on the ice after just 65 hours' flying.

The three men had loaded all their equipment onto the three sledges and set off for one of two emergency bases, set up with this kind of situation in mind. Conditions were so terrible they were making only a few miles a day, across ice floes which were drifting slowly in the opposite direction. After two months they reached the shore of White Island, where they decided to sit out and wait for the following summer. With enough food and fuel, their chances were reasonably good. But, due to unimaginable cold, and perhaps the effects of infected bear meat, they died within weeks.

The flight of the *Norge*

Even with the advent of more controllable airships, Arctic exploration held terrible traps for those who tried to fly over the frozen wastes. In 1926 the N1, an Italian semirigid airship with a central keel and a flexible envelope, was chartered by the Norwegian explorer Roald Amundsen and his financial backer, the American James W. Ellsworth, for a flight to the North Pole. The ship was renamed *Norge* (*Norway*) for the trip, and carried a skeleton crew of six Italians, including the commander, Colonel Umberto Nobile.

By 7 May 1926, the airship had arrived at King's Bay in Spitzbergen, ready for a planned flight across the North Pole and southwards to Nome in Alaska. Four days later, it took off and reached the Pole in 17 hours, where the crew dropped Norwegian, Italian, and American flags onto the ice. The *Norge* then set

BELOW: *The* Norge *drops flags as it crosses the North Pole, in this advertisement for a French producer of canned meat extract*

RIGHT AND BELOW: **Norge** *sets out for the Arctic in 1926 (right) and arrives at King's Bay on the island of Spitzbergen (below)*

course for Alaska, but ran into dense fog, while ice condensed on the structure and the envelope, and the compasses were useless because of the closeness of the magnetic Pole.

In the end, the airship made it as far as a frozen lake 56 miles north of Nome, when Amundsen insisted on a landing. They managed a smooth touchdown, and pulled the gas-release cords to deflate the airship. They had very nearly reached their destination, after a flight of 3,400 miles, but the ensuing publicity caused sharp differences of opinion between Nobile and Amundsen, who each accused the other of incompetence (see box on page 69).

This dispute convinced Nobile, now promoted to general, that he should prove his point by mounting a second expedition, under entirely Italian control. He adapted a new airship, of similar size to the *Norge*, which was to be named *Italia*, and planned a series of flights from Spitzbergen to the nearby Arctic coasts and on to the Pole. The expedition landed at their King's Bay base in May of 1928, two years after the *Norge*'s flight, and the program began with flights to other islands in the vicinity.

Back to the Pole

The Polar flight began at 01.38 GMT on 23 May, with the *Italia* flying northwest to pick up the Greenland coast, cruising on two of its three engines. Helped by a brisk tailwind, it reached the Pole at 12.20 am on 24 May. Once again, flags were dropped, including the standard of the City of Milan, which had helped back the expedition, a small medallion of the Virgin Mary, and a wooden cross given to Nobile by Pope Pius XI before the expedition left Italy for the Arctic.

After an hour over the Pole the weather began to worsen, so it was decided to turn back for King's Bay. Unfortunately, the tailwind was now against them, and ice was building up on the outer skin of the airship. With the airship becoming heavier, and the wind

Deadly rivalry

In spite of their successful collaboration in the flight of the *Norge* over the Arctic, Colonel (later General) Umberto Nobile and the Norwegian explorer Roald Amundsen became enemies. Nobile complained that Amundsen had contributed nothing to the trip, and its success had been due entirely to his airship, and his skill at commanding it. Amundsen countered by accusing Nobile of inexperience with Arctic conditions, and with dangerous incompetence.

Nevertheless, when Nobile's *Italia* crashed on the ice, Amundsen was quick to offer his help. With his fellow Norwegian Lief Dietrichsen, he joined the three-man crew of a French Latécoère flying boat. They took off to join the air search, and were never seen again. A man who had survived years of exploration in the toughest of Polar conditions had died in going to the rescue of his sharpest critic and deadliest rival.

Though Nobile had protested to be allowed to remain at the camp until all his men had been rescued, his injuries had resulted in his being taken away against his will. For all his efforts, he was court-martialed on his return to Italy for dishonoring his country. He went into exile, first in Russia and then in the United States, where he worked as an airship designer. He finally returned to Italy in 1943 after the overthrow of the Fascists and the repeal of the judgment against him.

ABOVE RIGHT: *Collaborators and deadly rivals, Roald Amundsen (left), first man to reach the South Pole, and Italian aviator Umberto Nobile (right)*

BOTTOM RIGHT: *Nobile's second and ultimately tragic Polar flight used another semi-rigid airship, the* Italia

freshening, the signs were set for disaster. At 6 am on 25 May, and again at 10, distress signals were received from the *Italia*, followed by total silence.

Half an hour after the sending of the second signal, the sinking airship struck the ice so violently that one of the engine cars and the main control gondola were torn off the structure. Freed of their weight, the airship, with seven crew members still aboard, rose into the storm and was never seen again. One mechanic died in the crash, but the other 10 survivors, including Nobile with a broken arm and leg, were forced to shelter in a tent, where they sent out desperate calls for help on an emergency radio transmitter salvaged from the wreck.

By the time rescue reached the camp on 17 June, in the shape of a Swedish biplane fitted with skis, three of the party—two Italian naval officers and an injured scientist named Malmgren—had set off across the ice to find their own salvation. The airplane could carry only one person in addition to its two-man crew, so General Nobile was taken back to their base, to help coordinate the air search being mounted by five different nations.

The Swedish pilot returned to the camp without his observer, to pick up more survivors, but crashed on landing, damaging the skis so badly that a take-off was impossible. This added another to the five explorers still awaiting rescue, though two weeks after the original landing the pilot was picked up when his observer managed to reach the camp in another plane on 6 July.

Russia to the rescue

It was now six weeks since the original crash and more than a month since three of the crew had set out across the ice to find help. As the weather worsened, making it impossible for other planes to locate or approach the camp, the situation looked increasingly bleak. Yet, unknown to the small group waiting patiently on the ice, the Russian icebreakers *Krassin* and *Malygin* were steaming through the fog toward them. During one break in the clouds, *Krassin* had been able to launch its spotter plane, which had detected the two naval officers walking across the ice, and the ship had picked them up. Dr Malmgren had had to be left behind on their journey, close to death, and his body was never found.

The very next day, *Krassin* arrived at the camp, and the five remaining survivors were safe at last. It had been a tragic and disappointing follow-up to the success of the *Norge* expedition, and the death toll was still rising. Apart from the four mechanics, the two journalists, and the scientist who had disappeared with the remains of the airship, another mechanic had been killed in the crash and Dr Malmgren had died on the trek across the ice. There was still worse to come. In the search for the survivors, a Russian plane from the icebreaker *Malygin* vanished with all its crew, as did a French flying boat carrying three Frenchmen and two Norwegians, Lief Dietrichsen and Nobile's arch-rival, Roald Amundsen.

Toward the edge of space

Ironically, as the limitations of airships were being revealed in expeditions to the remote Arctic regions, there was a renewal in the use of balloons to explore the equally daunting environment of the upper atmosphere, miles above the earth. As early as the fall of 1862, the English balloonists Glaisher and Coxwell had taken a gas balloon up to almost 30,000 feet and very nearly died in the attempt, from cold and oxygen starvation.

Their record had been broken in 1901 by a German meteorologist, Arthur Berson, who used a hydrogen balloon to carry him to a height of 35,000 feet where he survived by breathing pure oxygen.

In 1927, the year before Nobile's disastrous Arctic expedition, Captain Hawthorn Gray of the US Army ascended in a hydrogen balloon fitted with the classic open gondola to the staggering height of 42,470 feet. Gray was breathing oxygen and dressed in an electrically heated flying suit, equipped with a parachute, which was a fortunate piece of planning. As he started his long descent, the balloon fell faster and faster through the thin upper atmosphere. Unable to arrest its plunge, he had to bail out and come back to earth independently.

Later in the year, Gray tried again. This time he reported by radio that he had reached a height of 44,300 feet. After that all messages ceased, and the balloon failed to return. The following day, a boy spotted the gondola hanging in a tree, with Gray's body inside it. Either his oxygen supply had failed, or his lungs had been fatally damaged by the huge drop in air pressure at these record heights.

What was needed was some way of preserving the balloonists' lives by maintaining them in air at normal pressure. The solution to the problem was the closed and pressurized gondola, first developed by a Swiss physicist, Auguste Piccard. He built a sealed spherical aluminum compartment which was painted black on one side, to absorb the sun's rays, and white on the other, to reflect them. It was slung below the balloon on a harness that was fitted with a fairly powerful electric motor, which could be used to turn the gondola relative to the sun, so that its temperature could be controlled by the amount of solar radiation it absorbed rather than reflected.

Piccard's specialty was the study of cosmic rays, streams of atomic and subatomic particles approaching the earth from deep space. These are absorbed by the atmosphere, so his objective was to ascend to an altitude where they could be closely observed at first hand. Like all high-altitude balloons, Piccard's seemed completely underinflated at low altitude. This was to provide enough space for the gas inside the balloon to expand as the air pressure dropped, without bursting the envelope. By the time it reached the intended altitude, it would assume the spherical shape of a normal gas balloon.

Piccard's first attempt, on 14 September 1930, was a total failure. The balloon failed to leave the ground because of insufficient lift, and the sense of disappointment was heightened by the professor's physical appearance. His high forehead and long hair had been covered by a strange padded wicker helmet, so that he and his assistant, Dr Paul Kipfer, were dismissed as eccentrics, rather than serious scientific explorers, with a genuine mission.

Higher and higher

It took another eight months for Piccard's reputation to recover. By May of 1931, he had fitted a balloon with a capacity of almost half a million cubic feet to his spherical gondola. On the 27th of that month, the balloon lifted off from Augsburg in southern Germany, and in just half an hour had reached a height of 51,775 feet. Then things began to go wrong.

First of all, the electric motor froze in the intense cold of the upper atmosphere. Second, it did so with the gondola's black side turned toward the sun, so that the temperature inside the compartment rose to threatening levels. Third, the gas-release line, intended to open the valve to allow gas to escape from within the balloon and start the descent, also failed to work. All the two men could do was wait for the sun to set, when the gas in the balloon would contract as the envelope cooled.

At last the balloon began to lose height. By then, a leak in the sealed capsule was allowing air to escape, but by the time the pressure dropped they were already down to a safer altitude. They finally landed high in the Austrian Alps, and had to abandon the balloon to scramble down the mountainside to safety and rescue. When they recovered their instruments, they showed the balloon had reached a new record altitude of 51,770 feet.

Auguste Piccard was determined to ascend still further into this challenging area, and work began on a new and improved capsule. Unfortunately, a test model exploded in the workshop when a pressure test was being carried out, killing two of his assistants. Nevertheless, Piccard was undeterred and a new balloon and gondola were ready on 18 August 1932, when he took off with Dr Max Cosyns from Zürich in Switzerland, with a target of 52,500 feet in mind.

BELOW: *A magazine cover celebrates Professor Piccard's pressurized gondola and high-altitude balloon landing in the Austrian Alps after reaching a height of 51,770 feet in May 1931*

ABOVE: *The spherical pressurized gondola of the* **Stratostat USSR,** *riveted from 12 sections of aluminum alloy, on show in the Monino Museum near Moscow*

Once again the balloon soared into the upper atmosphere, and once again it drifted southward across the Alps. Radio messages from Piccard and Cosyns revealed they were encountering problems with the bitter cold, but that otherwise all was well. At last, after a day and a half on the threshold to space, the balloon came down safely on the southern shore of Lake Garda, in northern Italy. The balloon's instruments showed they had reached another record altitude of 54,789 feet.

Others join the race

Piccard's records did not stand unchallenged for long. In September 1933, just over a year later, the Russian balloonists Georgi Prokofiev, Konstantin Godunov, and Ernst Bernbaum soared to an altitude of 58,700 feet in the Soviet balloon *Stratostat USSR*. The United States responded with a pressurized-gondola balloon called *Century of Progress*, carrying Lieutenant Commander Thomas Settle and Major Charles Fordney to a height of 61,000 feet in November 1933.

The next round in this increasingly close race went to the Russians in January 1934, with the balloon *Ossoaviakhim* carrying a three-man crew to a height of 72,178 feet. Sadly, during the descent the pressurized capsule became separated from the balloon, and the crew were all killed in the resulting crash.

Ironically, a similar disaster nearly overtook the entire crew of the next American high-altitude balloon *Explorer I*, which had an envelope capacity of a full 3 million cubic feet. This took off on 28 June 1934, but the balloon had just passed a height of 61,000 feet when the crew saw to their horror that the envelope was beginning to tear. Immediately they started releasing gas from the envelope to begin their descent, but the tear continued to worsen before their eyes.

Finally, when they were still more than a mile above the earth, the envelope ripped apart completely, and the gondola went into free fall. Only because the balloonists were all equipped with parachutes were they able to open the hatch and bail out to safety, as the capsule plunged to earth.

Finally, two of the balloonists who so narrowly escaped with their lives from *Explorer I*, Captains Albert Stevens and Orvil Anderson, returned the following year to ascend in a still larger high-altitude balloon, *Explorer II*. This had a total capacity of 3.7 million cubic feet and was prepared at a special camp near

Farther into space

After the war, the United States high-altitude balloon program was revised, with a different set of objectives. This time, the balloons were to find out more about the upper atmosphere to pave the way for the coming space effort. For example, Major David Simons, a US Air Force doctor, spent almost two days in a pressurized capsule at a height of more than 101,000 feet in 1957, to check the physical effects of altitude.

Between 1959 and 1960, Captain Joe Kittinger made a series of free-fall parachute drops from heights ranging up to 108,200 feet to test pressure suits and parachutes for aircrew bailing out at high altitude. On one occasion he passed out because of violent rotations in free fall and was saved by his automatic emergency parachute, and on another he survived a fault in his pressure suit. Finally, in May 1961, US Navy Commanders Ross and Prather flew to a height of 113,740 feet to test the specially-designed suits soon to be issued to the Mercury space program astronauts.

Rapid City in South Dakota called the "Stratobowl." It took a fleet of 40 lorries to deliver 1,475 bottles of compressed helium to inflate this enormous craft to just one-fourteenth of its total capacity, which would be enough to raise it to the altitudes where the gas would expand to fill the envelope completely.

On 11 November 1935, the balloon stood a full 315 feet tall from the gondola to the top of the envelope. It left the ground at four in the morning and, by just after midday, the instruments showed they had reached a new record altitude of 74,185 feet. However, once again the technology proved fallible. There was a small leak in the capsule which was allowing oxygen to escape, and the flight had to be cut short. The balloon reached the ground safely after 8 hours 13 minutes in the air, and having traveled 125 miles from its starting point. Among the scientific experiments on board was a means of collecting samples from the upper atmosphere, which were found to contain certain types of spores. These were then grown and developed at ground level.

Blimps at war

When the US Navy had stopped its development of large rigid airships, following the loss of the USS *Macon*, only one kind of military airship remained on the books. This was the nonrigid airship, popularly known as the "blimp," which maintained its shape by ballonets inside a gas-filled envelope, rather than a rigid framework. The navy's first "blimps" appeared during World War I, based originally on British nonrigid airships, when their slow speed, long endurance, and relative reliability made them ideal for antisubmarine patrol.

The B class of nonrigid airships had gondolas made from modified airplane fuselages, and two of them were able to attack German submarines trying to lay mines in the approaches to New York Harbor in 1917. The later C class proved even more successful, and in May 1919 the C5 very nearly succeeded in becoming the first airship to make an Atlantic crossing. Forced to turn back after battling winds for nearly 25 hours, the airship was moored in Newfoundland, when it vanished in a storm.

BELOW: *The* Explorer II *lifts off from the "Stratobowl" in North Dakota on 11 November, 1935.*

BELOW LEFT: *A US Navy patrol blimp hitches a ride, by passing a towline to an American submarine*

RIGHT: *Six Goodyear-built "K" class patrol blimps in their huge hangar at the Naval Air Station at Santa Ana, California*

ZMC-2—the "Tin Bubble"

One nonrigid airship was built with the normal fabric envelope replaced by one of thin duralumin sandwiches, each one with a central layer of duralumin alloy between two sheets of pure aluminum. These panels were sealed together with over 3 million rivets to create a gas-tight structure.

This was the US Navy's **ZMC-2**, with a total capacity of 203,900 cubic feet and which was shorter and fatter than most orthodox blimps. Eight control fins were fitted to the tail instead of the usual four. It made its first flight in August 1929, and proved highly reliable in service. In 10 years of operation, it wore out its original engines, and replacements had to be fitted.

During the years between the wars, when the Zeppelin works was barred from producing airships, Goodyear acquired the Zeppelin patents, and started building a whole series of civilian blimps, as a way of gaining experience before switching to large super-luxury rigid airships. These varied in size from 57,000 cubic feet to 178,000 cubic feet, and all of them had gondolas faired into the balloon envelope as on the rigid airships. Helium gas was used throughout, and the blimps proved extremely reliable. They were used as airborne advertising signs, and as small passenger carriers. In all, the first of these civilian blimps made an overall total of 465 flights, and between them the fleet carried some 400,000 passengers without a single recorded accident.

It was this high level of safety and reliability that saved the military blimps when the big airship program was canceled. By the outbreak of World War II, several of the Goodyear fleet had been called up for military service as trainers for crews of the large numbers of the new "K" class of patrol airships (see box on page 74). In all, 135 of these were built for a wide range of duties, but most were used to escort slow-moving convoys and to help keep enemy submarines at bay. Six of the class were ordered to operate from North Africa in 1944, when they became the first nonrigid airships to cross the Atlantic, flying as a group from Massachusetts to Morocco, via Newfoundland and the Azores, taking a total of 58 hours for the trip.

After the war, new classes of blimps were equipped with radar to operate as fighter-control and early-warning airships. The largest of these were four ZPG-3W airships, which proved to be the largest nonrigid airships ever built, with a capacity of 1,516,000 cubic feet. These were introduced from 1958 onward, but a change of policy meant they would be the last military airships ordered for the US Navy. Finally, it took a disaster to bring about the closure of this airship program too. In June 1960, one of the four collapsed in mid-air over the Atlantic and was lost along with all crew members. A year later, the navy announced the ending of airship operations.

RIGHT: *A US Navy airborne early warning (AEW) blimp takes off in cold weather*

RIGHT: *AEW patrol blimps moored to wheel masts for easier ground handling*

The submarine that fought back

Only one US Navy patrol blimp was lost in action. This was airship K74, which detected the German submarine U134 on its radar screen at midnight on 18 July 1943. The U-boat was surfaced some 30 miles off the Florida Keys.

Because Allied merchant ships were passing through the area that night, the skipper of the airship disobeyed standing orders to attack the submarine. The submarine's anti-aircraft guns punctured the envelope and the blimp settled on the surface of the sea, where all the crew save one were later rescued by a US Navy destroyer. But the U134 dived and escaped, to be sunk on its homeward voyage by British bombers, while the merchant ships were saved from attack by the blimp's actions.

Unmanned balloons at war

Even unmanned balloons had a role to play in World War II. Though observation balloons had proved too vulnerable to enemy fire, massing large numbers of balloons together could create what was called a balloon barrage. The mooring cables of this array of balloons proved a deadly barrier to low-flying aircraft. In darkness enemy aircraft might be brought down by flying into these cables, and in daylight they could be forced to fly at higher altitude, where their bombing accuracy would suffer, and they would be more vulnerable to anti-aircraft gunfire.

The Japanese developed an unmanned bomb which could actually act as a bomber in its own right. The so-called *Fu-Go* balloon bombs were launched from Japan on the prevailing winter winds, which were intended to carry them over the United States. The balloons had envelopes of silk and tissue paper, mass-produced by schoolchildren, and they carried a mixture of incendiary and antipersonnel bombs. In all, more than 9,000 of these balloon bombs were launched, but only a few reached populated areas of the US. The only casualties were a woman and five children in Oregon, who found one of the bombs, which exploded when they tried to pull it out of the trees.

THIS PAGE: *World War II barrage balloons (bottom left) were similar in shape to the kite balloons used for observation in the previous war (top right)*

BOTTOM RIGHT: *Barrage balloons on the south coast of England deter German raiders in 1944*

TOP CENTER: *The Japanese "fu-go" pilotless balloon bomber of World War II*

5. Rebirth of the Hot-Air Balloon

By the late 1950s, and the sudden boom in long-distance air travel that came with the introduction of jet airliners, lighter-than-air flight began to appear as an idea whose time had gone. The style and luxury of the huge, rigid airships had perished in the flames of the *Hindenburg*, and even the smaller and more practical nonrigid blimps had outgrown their military applications. So far as balloons were concerned, the few survivors were almost all gas balloons, from the handful of scientific balloons to the even rarer sporting balloons. Whether filled with coal gas, hydrogen, or helium, the sheer cost of inflating a balloon was bound to keep ballooning a sport for the few.

This was in itself no surprise. From almost the very beginning of the development of the balloon, the gas balloon had taken the lead in popularity and practicality over its slightly older predecessor, the hot-air balloon of the Montgolfiers and their successors. The exploits of gas balloons, in wartime observation and peacetime exploration, had generated a lengthening list of achievements. As a result, little had been seen of the hot-air balloon for more than a century. It symbolized little more than a historical curiosity, a clumsy if essential stepping stone on the road to lighter-than-air flight.

Yet the ballooning world was on the verge of a revolution. Not the usual kind of revolution which sweeps away the old order and replaces it with the new: this would make an almost unprecedented step backward into history. Thanks to new technology and new materials, the oldest balloons of all would not only reappear in the sky, but would make the delights of ballooning far more accessible to all. Ballooning would become more reliable, more affordable, and more popular than ever before.

Not that this was apparent when the revolution began, in 1956. The trigger that set off the whole process was a US Navy research program, intended to find a more cost-effective way of providing the

ABOVE: *Ancestor worship: a modern hot-air balloon pays tribute to the first Montgolfier flight more than two centuries before*

BELOW LEFT: *Gas balloons being inflated for a competitive event at Tabor, Czechoslovakia in 1985*

BELOW RIGHT: *For more than a century, the shape of sporting ballooning was the perfect sphere of the gas balloon*

initial free-balloon training for future pilots of navy blimps. As this involved expensive helium balloons, the first step was to determine how an existing envelope would perform with hot air rather than helium as the means of generating lift. A Minneapolis-based company called General Mills was given the contract, and their work resulted in the first modern hot-air balloon to take to the skies in more than a century (see box on page 82).

But the catalyst which succeeded in turning this first hesitant experiment into a new way of leisure flying for a huge worldwide market was due to a different research project for a different service. Both the US Air Force and the US Navy was concerned about the problems of rescuing downed pilots over hostile territory, where landing a plane or even a helicopter might be impossible. One idea, called the PASS, for Pilot Aerial Survival System, was based on providing each aircrew member with the materials to make a small hot-air balloon, capable of lifting one person to an altitude where they could be snatched to safety by a specially equipped slow-flying airplane or helicopter.

The target was to devise a reusable balloon which could lift a man to a height of 10,000 feet and continue flying for three hours. The contract was awarded to a company called Raven Industries, based at Sioux Falls in South Dakota, which had been started by former General Mills researchers, and the team based their work on finding new materials and techniques for making the principles first established by the Montgolfiers easier to use and more reliable in action.

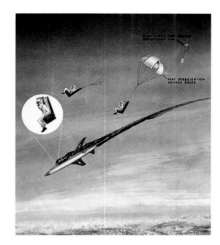

ABOVE: *How the pilot-rescue hot-air balloon project was supposed to work, lifting the crew of a crippled airplane high enough to be picked up by a special rescue aircraft, instead of dropping to earth on a normal parachute*

New materials, new ideas

First and foremost, they needed a new material for the actual envelopes of the balloons. This had to be light, tough, and fire-resistant, with a close enough texture to prevent the air inside it from escaping. After an examination of modern synthetic materials, they selected a light, woven nylon cloth which was ideal for the purpose except for one drawback. It was still possible for air to escape between the woven fibers, so that a plastic coating had to be laminated to its inner surface.

The second big question was how to provide the hot air to make the balloon fly. Some form of directional burner was needed, which could heat a large volume of air quickly to inflate the envelope, and then to persuade the balloon to climb, once it was inflated. This meant a high-energy fuel, which could be carried in containers within the balloon gondola, or basket. Kerosene and gasoline were both considered as fuels, but both needed to be pumped to maintain pressure, and the burners needed to be warmed up first, to provide the kind of flame intense enough to heat large quantities of air quickly.

Fortunately, tests showed that liquid propane, held in strong pressurized containers, needed no additional pumping to maintain a decent flame. Initially, the burners were surrounded by a metal baffle to prevent a gust of wind blowing out the flame. Later this was replaced by lengths of stainless-steel tubing, coiled around the flames, through which liquid propane emerged from the containers under pressure when

the boost valves were opened. When these tubes were heated by the flames, they helped the gas to vaporize more quickly. With this improvement, the burners soon proved powerful enough to inflate the balloon quickly and provide more sensitive height control.

Eventually, after a painstaking series of test flights, improvements to the design, and more tests, the initial requirements had been met by the end of 1969. Nevertheless, the idea of a DIY hot-air balloon as part of every aircrewman's escape and evasion kit never progressed any further. But the small band of researchers and developers soon came to realize that, as an unexpected bonus from their efforts, they had invented the first truly practical and highly economical sporting balloon.

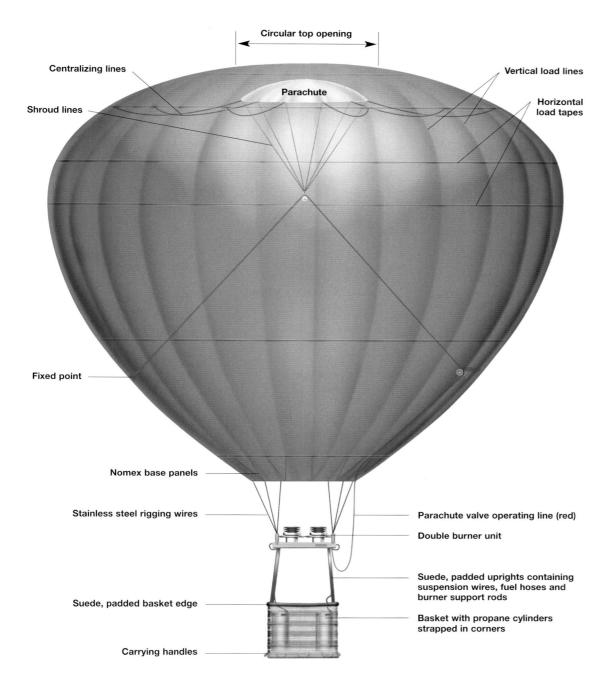

Circular top opening

Centralizing lines

Vertical load lines

Parachute

Horizontal
load tapes

Shroud lines

Fixed point

Nomex base panels

Stainless steel rigging wires

Parachute valve operating line (red)

Double burner unit

Suede, padded uprights containing
suspension wires, fuel hoses and
burner support rods

Suede, padded basket edge

Basket with propane cylinders
strapped in corners

Carrying handles

LEFT: *Construction details of a modern hot-air balloon. When the balloon is fully inflated, the internal parachute valve is held against the top of the envelope by air pressure, so that pulling on the valve operating line causes hot air to be vented through the top opening*

Using the combination of ideas and materials developed originally for this military requirement, they had reinvented the hot-air balloon, in a form that made immediate sense for a whole new generation of balloonists. Their ideas burst on the ballooning world like a revelation. Instead of fragile paper, silk, or cow's intestines, here was an envelope of up-to-date materials which was tough and strong, airtight and fire-resistant. Instead of a heavy, cumbersome, and dangerous furnace burning rotten meat, wood, and straw, the hot air needed to make the balloon rise was obtained by simply opening a valve to generate a large and powerful flame in an instant.

Here was a hot-air balloon that could be inflated quickly, controlled with great precision in the air, and flown for long distances. After landing, it could be stowed away in a compact enough package for an average station wagon. Perhaps even more important was the running cost, estimated at roughly 1 percent that of an equivalent gas balloon. Suddenly, the inspiration that had first made lighter-than-air flight possible had returned to the sky, making it seem a much more welcoming and inviting place for would-be balloonists. The challenge of balloon flight was reborn.

OPPOSITE TOP LEFT: *The open throat and the burner coils of a present-day hot-air balloon*

OPPOSITE TOP RIGHT: *Directing a jet of hot air into the balloon envelope during inflation*

OPPOSITE BOTTOM LEFT: *Mass take-off at a hot-air balloon rally*

OPPOSITE BOTTOM RIGHT: *The huge volume of the balloon envelope dwarfs the figures of its crew as they start the inflation drill*

Today's hot-air balloon

The familiar tapering shape of today's hot-air balloon, like an inverted raindrop, was developed during initial tests for the US Navy project. In other respects, though, present-day balloons inherit many of the features developed by pioneers of the nineteenth century. As with the earliest hot-air balloons, the main stresses are carried by the envelope itself rather than by the netting used with hydrogen balloons. To help the fabric cope with these loads, a series of horizontal and vertical reinforcing tapes run around the envelope rather like lines of latitude and longitude.

Long ago, balloonists came to rely on a means of opening the top of the balloon to let the lifting gas escape quickly when they wanted a sure and reliable landing. Present-day balloons still have this opening

The first flights

At the time of the Montgolfiers, very little was known about the ideal shape for a hot-air balloon. Because of the need for an opening at the bottom for the heat to enter the envelope, the hot-air balloon could not assume the perfect sphere of Charles's hydrogen balloon, and almost every gas balloon made since. So General Mills decided to approach the problem from the opposite end. They took an existing helium balloon with a capacity of some 27,000 cubic feet, which was filled with hot air and loaded with 450 pounds of ballast.

The balloon's shape was photographed, and studied. It had distorted from the original sphere to the inverted droplet so familiar today. The research team then fashioned the envelope of the next balloon, with a 30,000-cubic-foot capacity so that it would take up that shape without distortion, and fitted a large opening panel to the top of the balloon, released by triggering a set of explosive fastenings. The sole passenger would be carried on a square wooden platform slung on cables below the balloon, and preliminary checks determined the amount of burner power needed, and the peak temperature of the envelope, both of which were well within limits.

The first free flight of the new hot-air balloon took place from Bruning in Nebraska on 21 October 1960. The burner system was only just powerful

enough. Although the balloon was charged with hot air generated by an aircraft heating system, a slight breeze cooled the outside of the envelope at a faster rate than the single propane-vapor burner could cope with. The team could persuade it to take off only by walking downwind until the envelope warmed up sufficiently for it to rise. It reached a height of 500 feet, and stayed airborne for 10 minutes.

Burner modifications and a move to the Stratobowl in South Dakota, site of the prewar high-altitude balloon ascents, resulted in a much more successful flight three weeks later. The balloon reached a height of 9,000 feet and, though the test pilot, Ed Yost, had difficulties with controlling its altitude, it stayed in the air for 10 minutes short of two hours.

The third flight, with the burner-control wheel replaced by a handle for more rapid turning on and off of the flame, solved the height-control problems once and for all. Finally, the fourth flight in the series without a pilot, but with an equivalent amount of ballast, showed that, when the burner ran out of fuel, the maximum descent speed still ended in a survivable landing. The reborn hot-air balloon was a viable prospect.

CENTER RIGHT: *Pilot Ed Yost and ground-crew before the first flight of the Raven Industries' experimental balloon at Bruning, Nebraska*

ABOVE RIGHT: *The second flight of the Raven balloon at the "Stratobowl," proved much more successful and the design originally established the familiar shape of today's hot-air balloons (top)*

at the top, which is sealed for normal flight by Velcro tabs which hold a panel in place as part of the envelope, until a tug on the ripcord causes the tabs to part and release the hot air.

Some balloons have additional valves lower down on the envelope, controlled by other lines to allow a controlled release of hot air for faster descents. The gondola is now a strong but simple wickerwork basket instead of the elaborately decorated accommodation of the early balloons, with the propane containers securely strapped into the corners.

The burner unit is slung below the envelope by a set of stainless-steel cables attached to the network of vertical-load tapes. The basket is connected to the burner unit by a set of padded uprights through which run the support cables, rods to hold the burner unit in place, and the fuel lines connecting the propane containers to the burner unit. Compared with the balloons of yesteryear, this is a tidy, efficient, and businesslike set-up.

TOP LEFT: *The line to the escape valve can be seen linking the basket to the inside of the envelope*

ABOVE LEFT: *The burner unit on a modern balloon*

ABOVE: *Flying at 12,000 feet over the Swiss Alps in a hot-air balloon*

The original balloonists had no aids to navigation, beyond their knowledge of their surroundings and their estimates of height and time. With no way of knowing the temperature of the air in the balloon, or how much longer their furnace would keep them aloft, or even how high they were, they were flying by their wits, reacting to changes and emergencies as they happened. In a craft where only one direction of flight is possible—downwind—anything that provides a little extra warning is a gift to be cherished.

Here, too, the new generation of hot-air balloonists enjoyed real advantages over the pioneers. Burners were fitted with fuel gauges and burner pressure gauges, to reassure balloonists on how much propane was left and how effective the flame was going to be when next turned on. A simple altimeter monitors the balloon's height over the ground, and another pressure-sensitive instrument measures the balloon's rate of climb or descent. Because turning burners on and off has a delayed-action effect, making the balloon rise or fall, or increase or decrease its rate of climb and descent, any revelation of these sometimes quite gradual processes is worth its weight in diamonds.

Taking off in a modern balloon

The flights of the first aeronauts showed all too clearly that ballooning was a chancy and unpredictable business, an activity definitely not suited to the faint-hearted. Yet many of their troubles, like those of trailblazers in all fields, were down to the limitations of their technology, the materials they had to work with, and their knowledge of the physical principles governing their flights. Today's hot-air balloons are still a world away from the undramatic turn-the-key-and-take-off utility of the light airplane. Nevertheless, the distance separating them from the struggles of their predecessors is almost as great.

BELOW: *A 4-place balloon basket and burner frame*

BELOW RIGHT: *A hot-air balloon at the World Nature Games, Parana, Brazil, 1997*

Some things have still not changed. A balloon flight of today, just like those of Charles, Montgolfier, or Pilâtre de Rozier, has to start with the inflation of the envelope. The transformation has come in how the whole process is achieved. Instead of having to hold the envelope on cables above a furnace, today's flights usually begin with the envelope being laid out flat on the ground, preferably in a fairly sheltered spot. The parachute valve is fastened in place with the Velcro tabs, and the basket is laid on its side with the burners facing into the open mouth of the balloon, and all the straps and rigging in place.

The first stage of inflation means forcing enough cold air into the envelope to hold it partially open for the burner to get to work. Some balloonists do this by persuading some of the ground crew to flap the mouth of the balloon up and down, while others help the whole process along with a powerful electric fan. Once the interior of the balloon is accessible, lighting the burners produces a fearsome jet of flame several feet long. Successive blasts on the burner heat the air within the envelope and slowly the vast bulk of the balloon begins to stir as it approaches its proper shape.

To begin with, members of the ground crew will have been holding down the top of the balloon, to keep it lying on the ground for as long as possible. But, as inflation continues, the balloon rises toward its normal attitude, and the burners have to be tilted farther and farther toward the vertical, to send the flames into the mouth of the envelope. Eventually the balloon becomes taut, floating above the now upright basket, and the moment of take-off approaches.

On a still day, with nothing more than the merest breath of wind, the passengers can climb aboard, while the pilot continues to increase the lift generated by the balloon by directing the burner flames into the envelope. Once the lift is sufficient to overcome the weight of the envelope, the rigging, the basket, and its contents, the balloon will leave the ground as the laws of physics take over.

TOP LEFT: *Inflating a balloon—the envelope spread out on the ground*

TOP RIGHT: *Directing the burner into the envelope to heat up the trapped air*

ABOVE: *Holding the envelope open to increase the flow of air*

In a fresher breeze, such a gradual take-off can cause problems. When a balloon is held down with a wind current blowing over its curved surface, a lift force is generated, similar to that created by the airstream flowing over the curved surface of an airplane wing. This causes the balloon to take off and rise into the breeze, whereupon it starts to move with the breeze and that relative air current dies away. The lift drops and so does the balloon, coming back down to earth at the same speed as the wind.

To prevent this happening, balloonists often follow the example of the great balloonists of the past, when faced with the same problem. Put simply, this means building up lift beyond the minimum needed for the initial lift-off from the ground. By using every available helper to add their weight to the basket, the balloon can be prevented from taking off until a large enough reserve of lift is generated. When, at a given signal, the entire ground crew lets go, the excess lift is enough to carry the balloon up like an elevator, well clear of the ground and any tendency to drop back to earth.

Across the English Channel—again!

One of the early enthusiasts for the new kind of ballooning had a highly respectable name in the history of lighter-than-air flight. Professor Auguste Piccard, who had pioneered high-altitude balloon flights between the wars, had retired from flying and devoted himself to his academic work, but his twin brother Jean had emigrated to the USA, where he continued making high-altitude flights. On 3 October 1934, with his wife Jeanette, he beat his brother's record to reach a height of 54,789 feet over Detroit. During the 1960s their son Don Piccard had become interested in ballooning, and in early 1963 a team that included Ed Yost and Don Piccard as copilots took a hot-air balloon to England to help popularize the sport.

Their intention was to re-create the flight of Blanchard and Jeffries, by flying a hot-air balloon across the English Channel to the coast of France. Once again, there was only a sketchy gondola, consisting of a wooden platform and a pair of propane cylinders strapped to it, but, at 7.45 am on 13 April 1963, Piccard and Yost lifted off from the English coast near the old harbor town of Rye and headed out across the English Channel.

They crossed the French coast near Gravelines, between Calais and Dunkirk, as the wind was blowing them to the east as well as the south. They traveled a total distance of 65 miles in just over three hours and a quarter, and they reached a maximum height of 12,000 feet. The whole flight was so straightforward it barely made the newspapers, and, as a means of persuading the world of the delights of hot-air ballooning, it was a failure. The huge increase in the popularity of ballooning was still some years off, but, to those who could compare the almost effortless flight of the new balloon with the desperate struggles of Blanchard and Jeffries to stay out of the water on their Channel crossing, Yost and Piccard's balloon was indeed a revolutionary craft.

OPPOSITE: *Balloons en masse: a meeting at Metz, France, in 1995*

TOP RIGHT: *Creating lift in a Zanussi balloon using the burners*

BOTTOM RIGHT: *Evidence of enthusiasm: balloonists' club patches*

THIS PAGE: *By cutting costs and increasing the availability and simplicity of ballooning, the invention of the hot-air balloon has brought the delights of lighter-than-air flight to a wider public than ever before. More and more people are now able to enjoy for themselves the spectacle, the silence and the serenity of effortlessly skimming the earth's surface in a basket suspended on wires, fabric, and a cushion of heated air*

The joys of flying

Once safely airborne, the hot-air balloon comes into its own. Though the air in the envelope begins to cool as soon as the flame is turned off, the power of the propane burner is great enough to balance the cooling effect by turning the flame on for five seconds, every 20 seconds or so. Turning the flame on for a longer period each time causes the balloon to rise, and turning on for a shorter period, or at longer intervals, allows it to descend.

Compared with the gas balloon, where only dropping ballast can cause it to rise, and only venting gas can cause it to fall, the burner handle is an efficient and versatile control system. If the burner is turned off completely, or even if it failed or ran out of propane, in normal conditions the balloon would descend at about the same speed as a parachute.

Apart from the roar of the burner during the brief periods when the flame is turned on, ballooning is still as quiet a way of flying as ever it was. Because the balloon is driven along with the wind, there is no apparent air current, and very little motion. Sounds from the ground can be heard surprisingly clearly, and in light breezes the speed of the balloon is low enough for obstacles to be seen well in time for avoiding action.

This is just as well. Because the hot-air balloon has to be much larger than a gas balloon to generate the same amount of lift, it weighs more and displaces a much larger mass of air. Both these factors mean that, in ascending and descending through the atmosphere, the hot-air balloon has much greater inertia.

In other words, it takes more effort to start it climbing to avoid a tall building or a set of power cables, and its rate of climb is slow enough for the pilot to have to think and watch a long way ahead.

As the balloon climbs through different layers of the atmosphere, the strength and direction of the winds may change. Changes in air current also happen in hilly country or built-up areas, as the breeze funnels around or between tall buildings. As the wind changes, the balloon's inertia takes time to overcome, and the envelope can be blown partly out of shape. In extreme cases, hot air can be forced out of the envelope, and the burners have to be turned on to prevent the balloon starting to descend.

These changes in direction also need to be carefully monitored. At the least, it can mean that the ground recovery team with the vehicles to carry away the deflated balloon at the end of the flight will be miles away from its eventual landing place. At worst, the change in wind could blow the balloon off its original predicted flight path and into danger areas such as mountains, lakes, or even areas of bad weather, such as thunder clouds where strong and potentially lethal upcurrents lie in wait for the unwary.

Coming down to earth

Landing a hot-air balloon is still, as it was for the pioneers, the most demanding stage of a flight, and still calls for the most careful planning. The ideal landing site is a large, flat, open field, free from any kind of obstructions on the approach, or on the landing site itself. If the breeze is making the balloon travel quickly over the ground, some additional shelter on the windward side of the field can make the eventual landing much smoother, and experienced pilots use all their skill and knowledge of the area to aim for the best landing place as early as they can.

Some pilots control the balloon to approach the landing site with plenty of height in reserve, then set the balloon to descend quickly at the right moment. This calls for a great deal of skill and experience to know exactly when to turn on the burner, and for how long to burn, to arrest the descent at the right

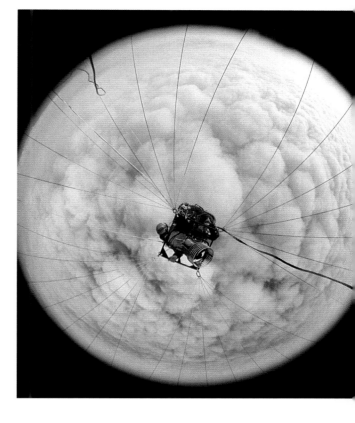

ABOVE: *Unusual view of a balloon crew, through a fish-eye lens camera mounted inside the envelope*

BELOW LEFT: *It looks like a 747 crash, but is really a "normal" landing for the Virgin Airlines advertising balloon*

moment for a smooth landing. Too little burning, or turning the flame on too late, and the balloon basket will hit the ground too hard. Too much burning, and the balloon may stop descending too early, and not touch down at all.

Others believe in starting the descent as early as they can, while avoiding any obstacles on the approach to the landing. The final descent may involve only one brief blast on the burners at around the mid-point of the descent, which will flatten the descent as the balloon nears the ground. As the ground nears, pilots use corrective blasts of the burner for fine-tuning the approach, and, if the landing is breezy, a tug on the ripcord just before landing, to spill the air from the envelope and damp down any tendency to take off again if any of the passengers fall out during the landing.

If conditions are calm, modern balloons are so tractable that they can be left inflated by using the ripcord carefully to spill some of the air. The basket can then be made to touch down gently, with the balloon still in shape for another ascent after a changeover of passengers or the loading of new fuel cylinders. With this kind of replenishment, a long-distance balloon flight can be prolonged over surprising distances, and the finesse of control allows competitive events to be set up that call for the greatest degree of flying skill and maneuverability.

Come the revolution

Perhaps the most surprising quality of the hot-air balloon is how long the revolution took to happen (see box on page 87). Suitable materials for the envelope and fuels for the burners had been developed some time before the US Air Force's search-and-rescue program triggered off the whole process. But, once the process began, its growth was truly spectacular. More and more of the new generation of hot-air balloonists set themselves up as makers of these apparently fragile but quite practical craft, and the whole process snowballed.

The more people saw balloons in flight, the more interest spread. Balloons appeared first as lone reminders of the past, over remote landscapes or crowded cities on days when the weather made flights possible. As their numbers increased, they appeared at events of all kinds from fairs and farm shows to specialized balloon competitions. They broke records and they spread advertising messages, all over the world. Most of all, they offered enthusiasts a link with a time when flying was both heroic and simple, when it had no objective other than that of pure enjoyment, riding the air currents to wherever the wind dictated.

By the early 1970s, there were perhaps 40 privately owned hot-air balloons in the United States, with around half that number in Britain and a handful in other European countries. Within a few short years, there were enterprising balloonists commissioning larger balloons generating enough lift for bigger gondolas and more passengers, so that non-balloonists could pay for their acquaintance with the sport. Balloon ownership went on rising, so that now their familiar shapes appear on skylines all over the world, and their numbers at major balloon meets in Europe and the USA create an increasingly spectacular airborne assembly. With more than ten thousand balloons worldwide, the revived popularity of the hot-air balloon shows no signs of ending.

TOP: *Crossing new horizons—a hot-air balloon over the inhospitable terrain of the Himalayas*

ABOVE: *Ballooning memorabilia: club pins celebrate the different shapes and identities of favorite balloons*

Balloons for parties

As the popularity of the new generation of hot-air balloons continued to increase, designers became adept at producing larger and larger designs, with greater carrying capacity. In a throwback to the public appeal of Giffard's captive balloons for the Paris World's Fair, tethered gas balloons had already been used to carry large groups of passengers aloft on captive flights. In 1979, the Dutch brewing company Heineken sponsored what was then the largest modern hot-air balloon, with room for 39 passengers in its doubledeck basket. Even this was overtaken by the still larger *Nashua* balloon, with room for 50 passengers, and the trend towards larger-capacity passenger balloons undoubtedly helped more people experience the joys of ballooning at first hand, creating a still larger demand for modern Montgolfières.

6. Balloons at Work and Play

With the ever-increasing number of balloons taking to the skies of Europe and North America, two subtle changes began to widen the appeal of these gentle giants of the skies. On the one hand, it was clear that the appearance of a large balloon in the sky almost anywhere was virtually certain to attract the attention of everyone in the vicinity. Moreover, it tended to hold that attention for the fairly long time the balloon remained in view, given the fact that most flights took place in relatively calm conditions.

All this made the hot-air balloon ideal as an advertising site. When shrewd organizations offered to sponsor balloonists with contributions toward the cost of building and flying their balloons, in return for the company name, logo, and slogans across the envelope, the deal seemed to offer a lot to both parties. More and more balloons appeared with the names and messages of every kind of commercial setup, as graceful airborne advertising billboards, and it seemed that everyone was happy.

From the advertisers' point of view, there was only one snag in this arrangement. No matter how carefully they designed their logo and pitched their copy, they were still stuck with the inescapable fact that all balloons looked the same. The awful possibility that the public might see a whole series of balloons and not remember the messages they carried was extremely worrying. Was there no way in which the balloon that carried their individual advertising could be made to stand out from all the rest, even at a crowded rally, when balloons were sailing past on every side?

BELOW: *Balloons need fairly still air to fly safely, and especially in the tropics this often means an early take-off before the land heats up and creates windy conditions*

The first shaped balloon—Robertson's Golly of 1976

Indeed there was, but the solution to the problem emerged only when balloon constructors gained in confidence over the flying ability of shapes that departed from the newly established norm. In 1976, balloon makers in Britain produced a design with a difference for Robertson's, an old-established firm of jam makers, based on their children's doll symbol, the Robertson's "Golly." This used a standard balloon shape for the head of the figure, with a long cylindrical body below it, and the basket slung below the "feet." With a black face, black and white eyes, red lips, and a blue coat, red trousers, white shirt, yellow vest, and a red bow tie, this was certainly a balloon that stood out from the rest.

Nothing succeeds like success, and a whole series of ever more bizarre and ever more ambitious shapes began to appear in the sky. The second shaped balloon was nothing less than a huge, disembodied pair of jeans, which owed nothing at all to the established shape of the balloon. The flat top of the envelope formed the waistband, while the basket and the burners were carried at the bottom of one of the legs, while the other leg was sealed at the bottom to prevent heated air escaping after early flights showed one leg apparently better filled than the other.

Shapes of every kind

After that, the introduction of computer software to simplify the cutting and shaping of the most oddly shaped envelopes made possible a whole new range of shapes. For a spark-plug maker, a tall thin balloon in the shape of a spark plug was a straightforward development. For a tire manufacturer, a balloon in the shape of a car wheel and tire standing upright was another logical symbol.

For one beer manufacturer, a beer mug was the shape of choice, while for another it was a can, but for a third it was the even more ambitious, and instantly recognizable, idea of a flying four-pack, which hit the target. Bottles of cologne, champagne, whiskey, and wine now join them at balloon events, together with a bouquet of flowers, a strawberry, and a bunch of bananas for a major supermarket chain.

At least two car manufacturers, Audi and Jaguar, have best-selling models echoed by balloon envelopes, with the bottom section of the envelope and the basket emerging from underneath. Another balloon portrays a Grand Prix racing car standing on its nose, another is an oil can, another a motorcycle, and another a steam locomotive advertising the Orient Express. Among the more unusual shapes, balloons have been produced shaped like a hand holding a mobile phone, a folded newspaper with columns of legible text, a running shoe, a black derby hat, a coffee pot, a roll of film, a house, and an Indian Taj Mahal.

Others are based on cartoon characters from Mickey Mouse to Sonic the Hedgehog, and on real and imaginary animals from tigers to polar bears, and from eagles to dragons. Add to the list a weeping clown, a laughing cow, a snowman, a cactus, a smiling sun, the head of Uncle Sam, a Halloween pumpkin, a Noah's Ark filled with animals, and a sky diver with parachute pack, smoke containers, reserve chute, and

oxygen mask, and it is clear there is apparently no limit to the ingenuity of the balloon makers in meeting the most extraordinary demands of owners and advertisers.

Only two problems remain for operators of these very special balloons. First, the more complex shapes can take a long time to inflate fully, for unless hot air reaches every section of the envelope before the balloon takes off, part of it may constrict and never fully inflate. This may not stop the balloon from flying, but it will spoil the carefully planned appearance in the sky. Secondly, when the flying is over and the envelope deflated, the task of folding it away to expel all the air and reduce it to a compact package without overstretching and distorting the shape on its next appearance is made much more difficult.

ABOVE: *Balloon meet at Chateau d'Oex, a highly popular ballooning center in the Swiss Alps*

Balloons in competition

Since the great days of the Gordon Bennet races, balloon competitions had tended to be confined to those with the bottomless pockets and limitless leisure needed to fly gas balloons across a continent to chase the longest-endurance flight. With the revival of the hot-air balloon, what was needed was a set of competitions that could involve the balloonists on a more immediate basis, and entertain the crowds for whom competitive ballooning at rallies was an increasingly popular spectator sport.

Part of the problem, as always, is that balloons drift only downwind, at the speed of the wind, so that racing in the ordinary sense is not really possible. Instead, competition is based on flying skill, in reaching as close as possible to a given landing mark, or in flying at different heights to make the best use of different wind currents to reach a particular objective.

These fall into a set of different categories. Many of them involve landing as close as possible to a cross marked on the ground by two strips of colored fabric. Others involve dropping a marker, usually consisting of a small sandbag with a colored streamer to make it easier to spot, either as close as possible to a cross marked on the ground by two strips of colored fabric, or down a "chimney" made of a very tall square-

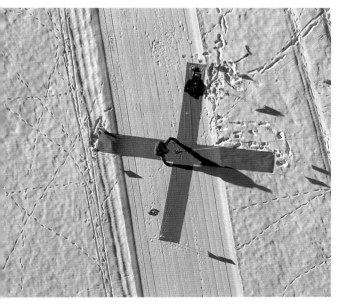

THIS PAGE: *A ground marker for a balloon race at Chateau d'Oex (bottom left) attracts more (top left) and more (top right) competitors as the event proceeds*

ABOVE: *A keen Japanese competitor throws out a marker which lands very close to the target*

section box, open at the top. Some events have what is called a "judge-declared goal," where the crosses and chimneys are placed by the organizers of the event, downwind of the launching site. "Pilot-declared-goal" events involve each competitor choosing their own targets before taking off, and then trying to place the marker as accurately as they can.

A variation on this theme is the Fly-in, where entrants start from anywhere they like upwind of the site of the event, and try to drop their markers on a target at the site. The similarly named Fly-on involves *two* targets, one compulsory, and the second chosen by the pilot during flight. This he writes on a marker, which he then drops at the first target. The so-called Hesitation Waltz also has two targets, this time as alternatives. The balloonist opts for one or the other during the approach flight, depending on the wind and the use he can make of different currents and different heights.

Another two-target competition is the Elbow, where balloonists try to make two flights involving the greatest change of course. They fly the first leg, and drop a marker, and then make maximum use of the fact that, as height increases, the wind tends to veer in a clockwise direction. By ascending and descending quickly, they try to make the second flight in a different direction before dropping a second marker, with the winner being the one who produces the greatest change of course on the two legs of the flight. Finally "Hare and Hounds" dates back to prewar days and the gas-balloon competitions, where a "hare" balloon takes off first, to be followed later by the "hounds," each of which tries to drop a marker as close as possible to the spot where the "hare" has landed.

The balloon that flies upside down

The best ideas are the simplest and most original, and, in the case of a machine-tool company called Festo, the idea was not to make an airborne lathe or power press.

Instead, the company name is carried by two perfectly ordinary-shaped balloons, with an identical blue and white color scheme and the company name and slogan. The only difference is that one of the balloons is flying right way up, and the other is apparently flying upside down, thanks to its inverted shape, upside-down writing and a false basket supported on a rigid framework at the top of the balloon, while the real basket hides in the inverted crown of the envelope. The result is an inspiration, an apparent disaster which creates an instant impression, whatever the surroundings, and a shape with an impact that's difficult to top. Except that someone, somewhere, will certainly be trying their hardest to do just that.

Single-seat balloons

For some adventurous spirits, even the restricted space of a balloon basket is too much. From the early 1980s, a new class of competition developed for small single-seat balloons of less than 42,000 cubic feet, where all the envelope has to do is provide lift for a single occupant, strapped to a tubular seat, with a single burner at the top of the seat back. Best suited to calm conditions, where the pilot can literally land on his or her feet at the end of a flight, these balloons offer the ultimate in miniaturization. With a framework that can be folded away into a surprisingly small space, and a propane cylinder that can double as an overnight case, many of these balloons can travel with their pilots to fly in other countries, without having to pay airline excess-baggage allowances.

However, perhaps the ultimate in personal balloons was represented not by a single, still relatively large balloon, but a whole lot of definitely tiny ones. One adventurous soul decided to go ballooning over California with a bunch of gas-filled balloons tied to a chair. For height control, he took along a revolver, with which to explode enough balloons to achieve the correct rate of descent when the time came. Unfortunately, he managed to drop the revolver early in the flight and had no means of controlling his altitude. Before long, air-traffic controllers were listening to airline flight crews reporting a man and a bunch of balloons crossing their approach paths into major airports, and fighters were sent up to investigate. It was only when the temperature dropped and the balloons started to lose lift, did he manage to return to earth safely.

ABOVE: *Walking a bar between two hot-air balloons calls for as much skill, if not quite as much daring, from the balloon crews as the bar-walker, to compensate for the transfer of weight from one balloon to the other. Recently this trick was repeated by a contestant in an audience-participation show for UK television*

BELOW: *Hauling a hang-glider to a suitable height for launching is another task where weight-transfer is critical, both at the moment of first take-off and at the final release of the glider and its pilot*

The terror factor

For many thrill-seekers, these contests of skill lack the sense of ultimate excitement, which can be provided by using balloons as platforms for all kinds of other challenges. From a very early stage in the balloon story, inventors of parachutes used balloons, literally, as jumping-off points to prove that their designs would work.

More recently, balloonists have allowed experienced parachutists to jump out of the basket at a high enough altitude for them to descend and be picked up again on the way down. This means reversing the tendency of the balloon to float upward at the reduction in weight resulting from passengers leaving the basket, and then putting it into a fast, controlled descent as quickly as possible. The parachutists deploy their steerable sport parachutes as soon as possible after leaving the balloon, and wait for the descending balloon to catch them up. They then aim for a safety net hanging below the basket, which allows them to spill the air from their parachute canopies and climb back aboard the balloon.

Other attempts to push the boundaries of the possible a little further include abseiling and bungee-jumping from balloons, and even a midair stroll by a tightrope walker between two hot-air balloons high above the earth. On this occasion the "tightrope" was a bar of aluminum, but the problems for the intrepid balloonists included having to compensate for the progressive transfer of the walker's weight from his starting balloon to his destination balloon without forcing him to walk either too steeply uphill or downhill.

More commonplace, in this world of balloons seen as launching platforms, is the lending of a helping hand to hang-glider pilots, hoisting them to a height they might find difficult to reach without the aid of thermals or mountain waves. This involves the balloon lifting off from the ground first, until it starts to support the weight of the hang glider and pilot, connected to the basket and burner frame by a support rope. With helpers holding down the glider until enough extra lift has been developed to carry the balloon and all its extra cargo safely clear of the ground, the whole combination then takes off and ascends to the planned height.

Thanks to the relative silence of balloon flight, the crew of the balloon and the hang glider can talk to one another, even if they cannot see one another. When they reach the launching height, the balloon pilot then turns the burner off and waits for the balloon to start descending, before cutting the towline and launching the hang glider. If the balloon was still climbing or even maintaining a steady altitude, there would otherwise be the danger of a fast and unplanned ascent as the weight of the glider and its crew was suddenly released.

Albuquerque, and the return of Gordon Bennet

The first National Hot-Air Balloon Championship in the USA was held in 1963, very soon after the concept had been proved all over again by Raven Industries. Within 10 years the sport had grown so quickly that the first World Championship was held at Albuquerque, New Mexico. The warm, dry desert air and superb visibility are ideal for ballooning, and the annual October gathering at Albuquerque sees what is almost certainly the largest number of balloons in the world to assemble at a single site.

There has even been a revival of the prewar long-distance Gordon Bennet races for the traditional gas balloons. These started again as an annual event in the USA in 1979, with competitors starting from Long Beach in California. Eventually races were held in Europe too, and after several years, when there was an American race and a European race, the event finally made its home in the Eastern Hemisphere.

Though technology and economics have greatly favored the new type of hot-air balloon, the Gordon Bennet events underline the survival of small numbers of traditional gas-filled balloons. Here new materials have had a less radical effect on the design of the balloons, though they have made ballooning easier. New fabrics are lighter, more durable, and more gas-tight than traditional materials. Their greater strength makes it possible to do without nets in some cases, and gas-release valves are now more reliable and easier to use. Yet gas balloonists still have the traditional ballast sacks and trail ropes that would have been familiar to generations of balloonists from the past, and still enjoy the almost unbroken peace of flight without even the periodic roar of a burner flame to disturb the silence.

7. Airships of Today and Tomorrow

The fiery death of the *Hindenburg*, and the quieter demise of the navy blimps, seemed to have drawn a firm line under the story of the dirigible balloon, which had begun so bravely a century before, with Giffard and the Tissandier brothers, Gaston and Albert. Yet the small, simple, and reliable nonrigid airship had three powerful advantages as an advertising vehicle. Its graceful and unmistakable shape provided the kind of spectacle that was impossible to ignore. Its large surface area was an ideal canvas for logos, slogans, and messages of every kind. Finally, it could remain in position for hours on end at a fraction of the cost and with none of the noise of a helicopter.

These advantages first became apparent during the 1920s, when Goodyear began building its series of nonrigid airships for publicity purposes, the later examples of which were taken over by the US Navy for training the crews of their wartime blimps. This same basic design was used again in 1968, when the company built two new nonrigid airships to extend the original series, carrying the names *Columbia II* and *Mayflower III*. A new, larger, improved version of the design, named *America*, was completed in April 1969, and all three airships used the latest materials and electronics.

Their envelopes were made from Dacron, a polyester fiber, and filled with helium, creating enough lift to support a streamlined control gondola with seats for a pilot and six passengers. Both sides of the envelope carried the company's "Super Skytacular" advertising displays. These were each made up of 3,780 red, yellow, green, and blue bulbs, interconnected with more than 80 miles of cable to produce animated color messages on the sides of the airship, controlled by a coded, pre-recorded tape edited in a computer laboratory on the ground.

These three airships, later joined by the *Europa*, which was reassembled in the UK in 1972 for flights over Europe, spent each summer traveling for thousands of miles to every kind of event. Between them, they popularized the idea of small and simple airships as a shrewd investment for any company or organization wanting to improve its profile with the wider public, and they played a vital role in the rebirth of this increasingly flexible and reliable lighter-than-air machine.

German airships

The Goodyear airships were not the only nonrigid dirigibles to be seen in postwar skies. As early as 1957, a joint venture between Metallwerk Friedrichshafen GmBH (the Friedrichshafen Metal Works Inc.), successors to the old Zeppelin company, and Ballonfabrik of Augsburg, had resulted in the building of a 154,000-cubic-foot nonrigid airship. This was broadly similar in size and design to the Goodyear machines, and was the first airship built in Europe to use helium for lift.

TOP: *Night-time advertising with the Super Skytacular bulb display*

ABOVE: *Checking and changing the bulbs mounted on the airship's outer skin*

In the early 1970s another German company, Westdeutsche Luftwerbung of Essen-Mülheim, built two more nonrigid airships, with 211,900-cubic-foot envelopes and gondolas with space for a two-man crew and up to eight passengers. One of these airships, the *Flying Japan*, was delivered to a Japanese customer in late 1972. The other, the *Flying Musketeer*, carried a German beer advertisement on its lower tail fin, and was also fitted with an animated light display on the side of the vast airship envelope utilizing a total of 10,000 bulbs.

Future possibilities

Among the varied names involved in different airship projects and operations around the world, one rings with a resonance that echoes back to the earliest days of commercial and military dirigibles. Zeppelin Luftschifftechnik is a subsidiary of the original company, and it stands out from its competitors on engineering grounds too. Where almost all postwar airship development has been concentrated on nonrigid or, in one or two cases, semirigid designs, Zeppelin capitalized on their unrivaled know-how to produce the first rigid airship for the best part of 60 years.

The company's NT07 prototype is big enough to carry 20 passengers, and made its maiden flight in Germany in September 1997. Production versions are currently being built, but the company's sights are set on larger versions for the longer term, more in keeping with their history. For the shorter term, a semirigid Zeppelin is also being built to carry up to a dozen passengers on short-range tourist flights for around $250 per person per hour.

A more ambitious project, which sets out to pick up the story where the wreckage of the *Hindenburg* dropped it, is the brainchild of Jonathan Hamilton, who has produced a prototype airship as a first step to building a massive 460-foot airship, just over half the length of the mighty German giant. Hamilton's target is to carry 60 passengers on intercontinental tourist flights, or up to 200 on shorter trips. Target date for completion of the full-size airship in South Africa was, at the time of writing, late 1999.

LEFT: *Goodyear advertising blimps publicizing the company name*

ABOVE AND TOP: *Return of the rigid airship and one of the most famous names in the business—Zeppelin's NT07 prototype (top) has a streamlined gondola, with room for 20 passengers and 2 pilots*

Biggest of them all—the Cargolifter

In addition to its potential for tourism and advertising, the other great virtue of a very large airship is its ability to lift and lower large or awkward loads without the need for transporting them to or from specialized ports or airfields, or fit them into the restricted dimensions of aircraft or container ships. Most ambitious of all the cargo-carrying future airship projects is the German semirigid Cargolifter, which is actually set to exceed the size of the *Hindenburg*, and cope with loads of up to 160 tons, which is well in excess of any existing aircraft around today.

Much of the difficulty and expense of designing and making heavy machinery is caused by the need to dismantle it for transportation and reassemble it on site. If the machine could be assembled once and for all at the plant where it was made, and then simply be shifted as a single unit to be dropped into place where its users want to operate it, enormous savings could be made.

This kind of thinking led a group of German engineers to look for a completely new means of lifting and transporting heavy loads. Though the resulting Cargolifter is an airship in all but name, the priorities are different from those that governed the design of the old Zeppelins. Here, generating lift is the main priority, and since each kilogram of lift needs a cubic metre of helium gas to lift it, the Cargolifter would actually be larger than the *Hindenburg*.

With an envelope containing almost 16 million cubic feet of gas, the Cargolifter would have more than twice the gas capacity, though because of its larger cross-section it would actually be slightly shorter. Lifting heavy loads would involve placing the load on a special loading frame which would then be hoisted up to the keel running under the envelope of the Cargolifter, as an equivalent amount of water ballast, collected from the engine exhausts, is released, to maintain a constant weight.

When the load was lowered at its destination, special water uptakes would reverse the process, to maintain the equilibrium of the craft as the load reaches the ground. The Cargolifter would not need to

RIGHT AND OPPOSITE PAGE: *Computer-generated impressions of the airship concept Cargolifter in action*

touch the ground at either end of its journey, and with a range of 6,000 miles and a cruising speed of up to 60 m.p.h. could outlift airplanes, outrun ships, and reach the most remote loading and unloading sites anywhere in the world.

At present, a one-eighth scaled-down prototype called *Joey* has already been built, and construction of the full-scale Cargolifter is planned to be complete early in 2000. The airship's home base will be in a specially constructed hangar on the site of a former military airfield at Brand, some 36 miles southeast of Berlin. The makers plan to launch the completed ship with a round-the-world trip in the style of the great Zeppelins, starting from the Hanover Expo 2000 and crossing Europe and Asia to reach Sydney in time for the Olympics and returning to base via the Pacific, North America, and the Atlantic. If the market lives up to expectations, Cargolifter's makers are confident there is no technical reason why the design could not be scaled up to make monsters capable of lifting as much as 500 tons in time.

RIGHT AND OPPOSITE PAGE, TOP: *Skyships over the Statue of Liberty and London's Tower Bridge*

BELOW: *Passenger cabin of Skyship 600*

The eye in the sky

In the meantime, the world's largest passenger airship, with room for two pilots and up to 13 passengers, flew for the first time in August 1998 at Elizabeth City in North Carolina. The nonrigid design is a Skyship 600, built and operated by Airship Management Services Inc., of Greenwich, Connecticut, and uses a new type of synthetic material for its 247,000-cubic-foot envelope.

Another feature of the Skyship design is a set of ducted power units which can swivel between horizontal and vertical positions to help the ship hover and maintain a position for long periods. These helped the airship set a new official world endurance record for time aloft without refueling of 14 hours and 10 minutes in September 1998, though an earlier example of the design set an unofficial world record over England of 52 hours, eight years before.

Variations of this successful design have been used for camera platforms (see box on page 108) for filming major sporting events like football matches and race meetings. One was sold to the UK Ministry of Defence in 1993 for high-altitude surveillance of terrorist activity in Northern Ireland, and another was used by the Woods Hole Oceanographic Institute for monitoring seal and whale populations. Airships have also been tested as observation platforms for anti-drug-traffic operations, and research is continuing into the development of "stealth" versions capable of carrying airborne early-warning radar for military purposes.

Another major airship operator is the Lightship Group, with a fleet of 13 airships and bases in Florida and the UK. These specialize in providing gyro-stabilized camera mounts, remotely controlled from inside the gondola, for covering the action at events like the Tall Ships Race, international golfing tournaments, and Major League baseball. The airships double as advertising hoardings, carrying company messages and logos, which can be illuminated from inside the envelope at night.

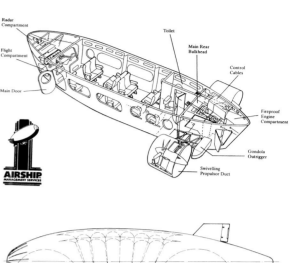

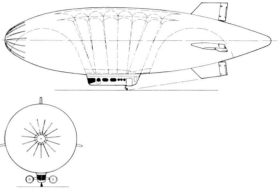

TOP: *The Skyship 600 gondola has room for 13 passengers, radar, and flight deck with toilet. It has two swivelling propeller ducts for lift and propulsion*

LEFT: *Site of the Low Altitude Surveillance System (LASS) airborne early warning airship operation at Yuma, Arizona. This airship has been used against drug smugglers operating across the southern borders of the USA, and also for detecting intruders across the Iraq-Kuwait border*

Pilotless airships

Airships have to be relatively large to generate the lift needed to carry a crew and essential payload—but, if the pilot can stay on the ground and control the craft by radio, then a camera-carrying airship can be made in model form. Since the early 1980s, a UK company, Airspeed Airships, has been building a range of remotely piloted camera carriers. The smaller types are compact enough to provide a bird's-eye view of indoor events held in large sports and exhibition halls, while larger versions can operate outdoors at heights up to 800 feet.

Because these camera platforms are quieter than the remotely piloted helicopter camera mounts, they have been used for filming wildlife, including close-up pictures of birds in flight. Other applications include low-level ground inspection in landmine clearance operations and monitoring the condition of remote parts of the exteriors and interiors of historic buildings.

TOP RIGHT: *Airspeed remotely-piloted electrically driven airship for wildlife filming in Africa*

RIGHT: *Old UK airship hangars at Cardington, home of the R100 and R101, taken from remotedly-piloted airship*

Communications blimps

Because the relatively cheap and simple nonrigid blimp can hover over a particular spot for a long time using very small amounts of fuel, they compare favorably with the cost of launching and maintaining communications satellites. Already Japanese engineers are planning to locate as many as 200 of these airship relay stations over Japan, at a height of some 80,000 feet, well clear of commercial airways, to relay signals from mobile phones and data transmission systems.

A US company, Sky Station, plans a similar network of communications airships on a worldwide basis. Each Sky Station would be located more than 65,000 feet above a major city, to relay radio signals over a ground footprint covering some 7,000 square miles. The first one is scheduled to lift off in 2000, and each one is expected to cost some $3 billion, which is around a tenth of the cost of putting a satellite into orbit to do the same job.

Over the skyline

Into the new century, it seems increasingly likely that lighter-than-air flight will continue to earn its place in the skies, even in the face of increasing pressure from the airplane industry. At present, relatively small nonrigid airships cost between half a million and 5 million dollars apiece, which has tended to limit their use in many applications where their virtues would make them more attractive at lower costs. An Alabama-based airship designer, Jesse Blenn, is confident that semirigid airships are inherently more efficient than nonrigid types, and that too much attention has been paid to using new materials, at the expense of the engineering of the airship structures.

The thinking behind the UpShip project is to produce a more agile and easily handled semirigid airship which uses a strong keel along its lower surface to allow a more aerodynamic shape and carry most of the stresses. Two engines would be mounted internally at the tail of the airship, with propellers directing their airstream over combined rudders and elevators, with a third engine mounted at the nose of the airship for additional maneuverability. The smallest version of the UpShip will use a small mooring mast mounted on a trailer or pickup truck, and can be handled by the pilot without the need for a large ground-handling crew, which is another expensive feature of some airship operations.

At the opposite end of the size-and-simplicity spectrum is the staggering AeroCarrier project, developed by a team from the design department of the Illinois Institute of Technology. This extends the weightlifting potential of lighter-than-air craft way beyond that of the most far-seeing inventors. It embodies a huge circular structure a mile and a half across, and would be capable of carrying 3,500 passengers, or 35,000 tons of cargo!

LEFT: *An artistic impression of the enormous AeroCarrier project for a circular airship, capable of lifting thousands of passengers or tens of thousands of tons of cargo*

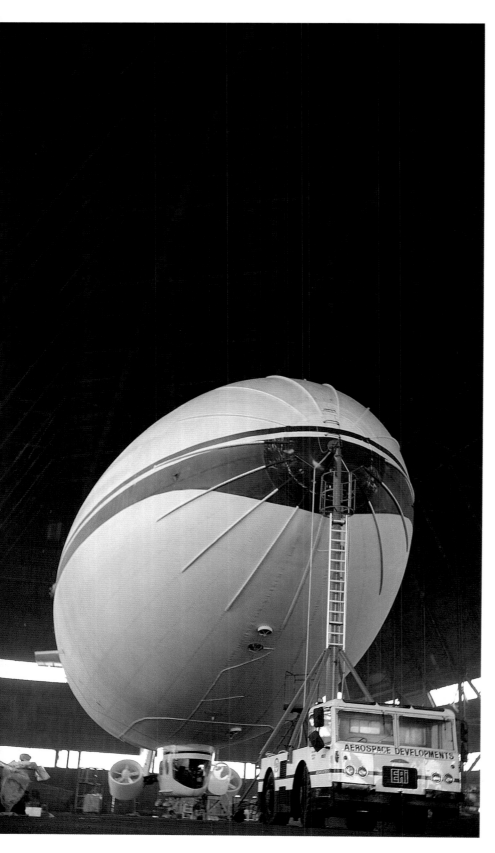

LEFT: *Modern airship inside the Cardington hangar (see picture on page 108)*

The future could be spherical

From the very dawn of the dirigible, it has always been assumed that the shape of the envelope needs to be long and narrow, compared with the sphere of the free-floating balloon, to make it stable and controllable. Even modern airships continue to rely on this assumption, with one exception. A Canadian company, 21st Century Airships Inc., has produced a series of six prototype airships which are almost perfect spheres. Not only do these lack the usual control fins mounted at the rear of a conventional airship, but they have no external gondola either. Instead, pilot and passengers sit in a cabin inside the outer layer of the double envelope, at the bottom of the sphere.

The spherical airship is controlled by two engines, each one mounted on a stub wing protruding from the outside of the envelope. When both engines run at the same speed, and deliver the same power, the airship moves forward or backward in the usual way. When the engine outputs are varied, the airship can be made to change course. By keeping one engine providing forward thrust, and setting the other to produce reverse thrust, the airship can turn in little more than its own diameter, much more quickly than the rather cumbersome maneuvers of a conventional blimp.

Altitude control also depends on engine thrust. Vanes are placed behind the engines. Tilting these vanes to deflect the engine thrust downward causes the sphere to rise. Tilting them to deflect the thrust upwards causes it to descend. The final prototype was named *Ball of Dreams* and is finished so that its 41,200-cubic-foot envelope resembles a giant baseball. It measures 43 feet across and, with a pair of 50-horsepower engines, can propel a pilot and passenger at a top speed of 37 m.p.h.

Now the company has completed a larger, pre-production model of just

over twice the size. Measuring 56 feet across, with a capacity of 92,000 cubic feet, this has four engines, a top speed of 40 m.p.h. and capacity for a pilot and three passengers in a cabin with a total floor area of 700 square feet. Windows cover almost half the circumference, with an access door at the rear of the cabin. A still larger 10-passenger version is scheduled for certification by mid-1999 for low-speed sightseeing trips over tourist centers like Niagara and the Grand Canyon.

Because the control surfaces generate their own airflow, the spherical airship does not have to generate forward speed to land or take off as a conventional airship does. It can also be moored by tying it to the ground, as its spherical plan means it does not have to weather-vane in the wind from an expensive mooring mast, like cigar-shaped dirigibles. Future projects include a cylindrical version of the concept, which can be customized to resemble a beer or soda can for advertising purposes.

Flying a modern airship

RIGHT, AND BELOW FAR RIGHT: *Modern hot-air airships are considerably cheaper to buy and to fly than helium airships, but lack their range and performance. The crew sit in a microlight gondola with a rear-mounted airscrew and an upward-oriented burner assembly set below an opening in the center of the airship envelope.*

BELOW CENTER: *The cockpit of an American "blimp" AB60*

Nonrigid airships have to maintain the right pressure within the envelope, which is done by air bags called ballonets. As the airship climbs and the outside air pressure falls, the helium inside the main part of the envelope expands. By opening valves to release air from the ballonets, the pressure can be maintained without losing valuable helium. When the airship descends and the air pressure rises, the helium contracts, so the pressure of the air in the ballonets is increased by using electric fans or diverting air from the propellers.

The same effects can be caused by changes in the outside air temperature. When sunlight falls on the outside of the envelope, the gases inside it are warmed up and expand, causing the pressure to rise. A colder airstream will have the opposite effect, and once again the ballonets are used to compensate for these effects. In addition, many airships have two ballonets, one at each end of the airship. Due to a variation in the air pressure between front and rear, the ballonets can be used to help trim the airship and make it fly level.

The pilot of a modern airship can also control the attitude and the movements of the ship with engines and control surfaces, just as with an airplane. By moving the controls to tilt the horizontal fins at the tail of the airship downward, the tail can be made to rise and the nose to drop, and the airship will lose height. Moving the controls in the opposite direction will cause it to rise. Turning the vertical rudders will cause the airship to turn to the left or right.

Airships whose engines deliver purely horizontal thrust have to accelerate once the mooring has been left, to the point where the airstream moving over the control surfaces allows the pilot to put the craft into a climb. This is similar to an aircraft taking off from a runway, but, since most of the lift is provided by the helium in the envelope, it happens at a much lower speed.

In the same way an approach to the mooring has to allow the ground crew to capture the airship before speed drops below the level where the flying controls become ineffective. These maneuvers become much easier when the engines can be tilted, or have additional control surfaces to provide vertical thrust.

Modern airships are inherently safe. Helium will not burn, and tests in which shots have been fired into the envelope have left the airship floating very gently to earth. Even engine failures leave plenty of time for the crew to achieve a smooth landing. Modern navigational aids and communications enable thunderstorms and turbulent winds to be avoided, and even snow settling on the upper surfaces of the envelope and adding to the weight can usually be dislodged by pulling ropes over the top of the ship while in flight.

Most working airships are kept inflated all the year round, moored to small portable masts. They need constant attention to keep them floating above the ground, by adjusting the lift through adding or removing lead weights, even when they do not fly. The envelopes are usually deflated only for regular inspections and safety checks.

TOP LEFT AND TOP RIGHT: *Modern advertising blimps are extremely versatile, like these publicizing a tour by the UK pop group Pink Floyd (top left) in 1994 and the Virgin Airlines service between New York and London (top right)*

ABOVE: *Gondola of an illuminated airship generating night-time publicity for Blockbuster Video*

8. Balloons to Girdle the Earth

Two centuries ago, the balloon seemed to offer the only real hope for humankind to leave the bonds of earth behind. A hundred years ago, that limitless promise had begun to tarnish, with a better appreciation of the limits of lighter-than-air flight. Fifty years ago, balloons and airships seemed but a stepping stone on the way to flight by heavier-than-air machines, staying aloft through a combination of engine power and fixed or rotary wings, instead of a gas-filled envelope. At best, balloons and airships seemed fragile and restrictive, the airborne equivalent of the sailing ship; at worst they appeared all too deadly.

Yet the latest stage of the balloon revival has seen developments that those early pioneers could never have visualized. Balloons have flown in the remotest parts of the world, and across the widest oceans, at speeds and heights that would have seemed impossible a generation ago. New ideas and new technology have extended ranges and capabilities by leaps and bounds. And, with a final touch of irony, the combination of hot-air balloon and gas balloon that took the life of Pilâtre de Rozier, ballooning's first hero and first fatal casualty, has proved the most durable and promising of all these high-technology designs.

Crossing the ocean

The old balloonist's dream of sailing effortlessly across the Atlantic, riding the prevailing westerlies from North America to Europe, remained an elusive and dangerous ideal for several lifetimes. Remarkably, one of the most promising attempts was the flight of the *Small World* gas balloon, which set out in 1958 from the Canary Islands, off the northwest coast of Africa, to fly the "wrong way" across the Atlantic from east to west. The balloon had a capacity of 60,000 cubic feet and carried a crew of four, but, in a prudent nod toward Professor Wise's *Atlantic* balloon of 1859, the gondola itself was adapted to serve as a lifeboat, should the balloon have to ditch in the sea.

It was just as well. The balloon sailed off over the sea, and disappeared from the world's attention for a matter of weeks. When the four voyagers, Colin and Rosemary Mudie and Arnold and Tim Eiloart, appeared again, they sailed the gondola into Barbados, reporting that their balloon had run short of gas and had come down in the sea after a creditable flight of 1,450 miles.

This proved to be a great deal more successful than a whole succession of west-to-east attempted crossings. Time and again a balloon would leave in a promising westerly breeze, only to ditch in the sea after covering only a fraction of the crossing. Sometimes the crew were rescued, sometimes not. In eight attempts, five balloonists died before Ed Yost, test pilot of the first modern hot-air balloon, left the coast of Maine in October 1976 aboard a gas balloon called *Silver Fox*.

Despite his experience, his balloon dropped into the Atlantic after being blown south of its intended course. But the attempt was the closest yet to success. *Silver Fox* had stayed airborne for 107 hours and 37 minutes, and in that time had traveled 2,475 miles to ditch 100 miles short of the Azores.

When the Atlantic *was* successfully crossed, it was to be in a balloon *made* by Ed Yost rather than one piloted by him. In August 1978, Ben Abruzzo, Maxie Anderson, and Larry Newman left Maine in the gas balloon *Double Eagle II*. They were able to drift north of Yost's track to cross the French coast, finally coming down less than 60 miles from Paris after a flight of 3,106 miles, which had taken 137 hours and 5 minutes, both new endurance records in terms of distance and time. However, both these new records would be broken by a succession of crossings within a few short years.

In 1984, the high-altitude balloonist and parachutist, Joe Kittinger, flew even farther single-handed, in a gas balloon that landed in Italy, after a flight of 3,544 miles. And in 1986 two Dutchmen also succeeded in crossing the Atlantic, and managed to end their flight in their own country.

Hot-air record breakers

So far, all the record-breaking long-distance flights had been made by gas balloons. But in 1987, the Swedish balloonist Per Lindstrand, sponsored by the British business tycoon Richard Branson, who had earlier crossed the Atlantic aboard a specially built power boat, produced the largest hot-air balloon in the world to make a different kind of ocean crossing. It had an envelope of more than two million cubic feet capacity, and a closed gondola with every kind of navigation and safety device.

In late June the balloon, named *Virgin Atlantic* in honor of Branson's companies, left New England with Branson himself aboard. All went well until they were approaching the British Isles, when a cold front over Northern Ireland appeared directly in their path. At this point, faulty batteries cut off their radio communications with the outside world, and, if the balloon did not manage to land in the worsening visibility, it risked being blown across Scotland, the North Sea, and Scandinavia, eventually crossing into Russia.

Lindstrand attempted a landing in Northern Ireland, as a rehearsal for a proper landing on the Scottish mainland, before they were blown into the mountains to the north of Glasgow.

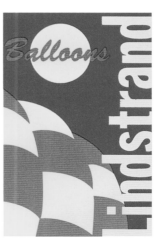

Unfortunately, as he was descending to make his landing approach, the balloon met the downdrafts of the weather front, and began losing height far too quickly. Turning on the burners to make the balloon climb, they made a heavy touchdown in a field just outside the small town of Limavady, near the Northern Ireland (Ulster) coast, before soaring back into the sky.

The weather grew steadily worse, with the cloud base descending to just 500 feet above the sea, and, with mountains ahead, Lindstrand decided to ditch in the sea as the lesser of two evils. They touched down in the Irish Sea, and detonated the explosive bolts designed to separate the floating gondola from the balloon. There was an ominous lack of response, caused by more battery problems.

There was now a danger that the balloon might rise again, and the bolts might detonate at any time, dropping the gondola into the sea from hundreds of feet in the air. Before this could happen, he shouted to Branson to jump into the water and did so himself. Branson stayed put, and, relieved of Lindstrand's

Return of the Rozière

One of the problems with long-distance balloons, whether gas or hot-air, is their sensitivity to changing temperatures. Although the hot-air balloon is immune to the problems of gas leakage that sooner or later limit the range of gas balloons, a hot-air balloon needs to be much larger to generate the same amount of lift, and therefore needs to carry a large amount of fuel, which adds to the weight that has to be lifted.

This combination of virtues and vices has led to one of the most extraordinary mutations in the evolution of the record-breaking balloon. This is the return of the combination balloon, or Rozière, which proved so fatal for Pilâtre de Rozier on his abortive Channel crossing two centuries ago. However, with the lethal combination of highly flammable hydrogen in a leaky envelope directly over an open furnace replaced by the best and safest of present-day technology, the Rozière has proved highly successful as a long-distance balloon.

Present-day Rozières have a helium envelope at the top of the balloon, providing most of the lift. Below this is a hot-air envelope, with an open end set over propane burners in the usual way. During the day, when the envelope is warmed by the sun, the helium expands to provide all the lift without the need for hot-air burners. When the air

cools at night, the burners heat the hot air below the helium, which provides extra lift and also warms the helium, keeping it expanded and

buoyant. Another advantage is that the Rozière combination can be a lot smaller, for a given amount of lift, than a pure hot-air balloon.

Rozière record-breakers

In February 1992, two Spanish balloonists, Thomas Feliu and Jesus Gonzales Green, set off in a 60,000-cubic-foot Rozière balloon from the Canary Islands, trying to succeed where the *Small World* had failed 34 years before. After covering 3,163 miles in 130 hours and 30 minutes, they completed the first Rozière

crossing of the Atlantic, and the first east–west balloon crossing, landing in Venezuela, South America.

The Rozière fashion had spread quickly. In September of that same year, five of these combination balloons, each with a 77,000-cubic-foot envelope and a crew of two, left Bangor, Maine, in a race across the

Atlantic. Two had to ditch in the sea, though both crews were rescued. The others completed the crossing successfully, one landing in Portugal, another in Spain, and the third, which covered the greatest distance, in the North African kingdom of Morocco.

weight, balloon, and gondola, Branson sailed off into the clouds, taking with him all the safety equipment.

Lindstrand was eventually spotted by a rescue helicopter which directed a launch to pick him up. Branson himself stayed aboard the balloon, which rose to 5,000 feet before descending gently into the sea. Because the emergency radio beacon had not been activated, he was extremely lucky to have been picked up by a Royal Navy frigate, especially since the gondola hatch had been replaced the wrong way round, leaving the craft to fill with water in minutes. Nevertheless, they had succeeded in crossing the ocean, and establishing a world endurance record for hot-air balloons of 2,788 miles.

Across the Pacific

In spite of the growing popularity of Rozière balloons for long-distance flights (see boxes on page 116) the next transocean attempt by Lindstrand and Branson—to cross the Pacific from Japan to North America—was to involve another huge hot-air balloon. This had begun badly, with bad weather postponing the launch from mid-December 1990 until 13 January 1991. Weather conditions were now good, but the balloon had only just taken to the air when Operation Desert Storm opened, with a massive aerial assault on the Iraqi invaders of Kuwait. This meant that US search-and-rescue planes would not be available, which added greatly to the danger of the crossing.

In the end, the flight lasted for almost two days. The balloon ascended to the altitudes of the high-speed jet streams, winds that blow steadily and relatively predictably around the earth from west to east, and it began flying very fast, in turbulent air conditions. Unfortunately, these high altitudes are very cold, and droplets of fuel froze around the burner jets. Eventually, these built up to the point where a mass of burning crystals fell onto the gondola, setting it ablaze.

Lindstrand managed to extinguish the fire by ascending still higher, but this took precious fuel. The shortage was made worse by the fact that two fuel containers had been accidentally dropped overboard early in the flight. Another problem was the direction of the jet streams, which were taking them north of their planned track. Finally, after 46 hours in the air, the balloon came down on the surface of a frozen lake in Alaska, some 2,000 miles away from their intended destination in California.

Over the Himalayas

In 1991, two hot-air balloons flew over some of the most challenging and dangerous country for lighter-than-air flight, in the jagged shape of the high Himalayas. They took off from Gokyo, Nepal some 15 miles west of Mount Everest, after the balloons, their fuel, equipment, and stores had been carried over precipitous mountain trails. One balloon, carried the specialist aerial film-maker Leo Dickenson and his Australian pilot Chris Dewhirst (pictured); the other carried the mountaineer Eric Jones and pilot Andy Elson.

The intention was to use one balloon to film the other, since the heights and the rate of climb and descent would be too great for a camera helicopter to cope with. In reality, the balloons became separated early in the flight, and only the most distant shots were possible. Nevertheless, Leo Dickenson carried a range of cameras—working from a small plywood platform outside the balloon basket—and another camera was slung from a harness below the envelope of the balloon itself.

The balloons flew to the north of the 25,850-foot peak of Nuptse, and the even higher 27,890-foot Lhotse before sailing across the summit of Everest—at 29,028 feet the highest mountain on Earth—at a brisk speed of more than 60 m.p.h. The second balloon was flying much lower, and over the Khumbu Valley the burners suddenly went out. Jones and Elson managed to get them relit, but when crossing the nearby icefall they went out again.

The balloon began to plunge downward. Twice more the burners were relit, and, to gain height to avoid colliding with the mass of the mountain downwind of them, all five burners had to be turned to maximum. This heated the wires holding the basket to the envelope, and three of them in one corner parted. With the grim choice of

keeping the burners going, at the risk of the basket parting company with the balloon, or turning down the heat and crashing into the mountain, they decided to keep the burners going, and cleared the ridge ahead of them, only to be shaken in the violent air currents on the lee side of the peak.

Finally, both balloons cleared the highest peaks, and sailed across the high plateau of Tibet. The Dickenson–Dewhirst balloon came down first in a crash-landing, short of fuel and spilling both of the crew overboard, after dragging Leo Dickenson upside down until his trapped boot came off. The balloon was finally retrieved three miles away. Meanwhile, the second balloon, despite the burner problems and the loss of the ripcord, which had been burned away, had more fuel left and was able to land in the next valley, so gently that the basket remained upright.

TOP: *The Jones and Elson balloon plunges downwards after the burners go out*

LEFT: *Dickenson outside the balloon, captured by a remote camera slung from the envelope*

BELOW: *The envelope of the 1997–98 Virgin round-the-world balloon takes off on its own from Morocco after an accident while it was being inflated*

Round the world

With more and more ambitious balloon flights being made over more and more difficult and dangerous territory, there was soon only one serious target still remaining: the first successful flight of a balloon right around the world. Richard Branson was determined to crown his successful Atlantic and Pacific Ocean crossings with the first circuit of the globe, and set off for Morocco in early 1997, though it was clear he would face determined opposition from at least two quarters. One challenger was the Swiss Breitling Orbiter balloon, which was to be piloted by Bertrand Piccard, another of the renowned ballooning family, together with Wim Verstraeten, who had already succeeded in an Atlantic crossing. The Orbiter had a tubular pressurized gondola with rounded ends, intended to allow the balloon to reach the altitudes needed to pick up the fast jet-stream winds.

The third contender was the American millionaire Steve Fossett, who had already made a 5,467-mile solo crossing of the Pacific from South Korea to Canada in a Rozière balloon in February 1995. For his round-the-world attempt, he would again be using a Rozière balloon, but with a classic open gondola, which restricted the height at which he would be able to fly, and therefore the likely range of his flight.

The first attempts showed how difficult the whole challenge was, even with the benefits of modern technology. The Branson *Global Challenger* balloon left Marrakech on 7 January 1997, but problems with equipment led to a disappointing flight, with the balloon coming back down to earth after only 20 hours and 400 miles.

On the 11th the Breitling Orbiter took off on its flight, but once again the technology got in the way. The balloon was using kerosene as a fuel instead of propane, since this would avoid the need for heavy pressurized containers for storage. Unfortunately, a leaking connector allowed fumes to seep into the gondola, and the crew ditched the balloon in the Mediterranean off the coast of southern France, within only a matter of hours of their take-off from their base in Switzerland.

The balloon that flew the farthest was by far the simplest. Steve Fossett's first flight had taken him from his home base in South Dakota to New Brunswick in eastern Canada. On 13 January he started again from St Louis, and in six days of solo flight he reached Sultanpur in northern India before a combination of worsening weather and extreme fatigue forced him to land, after covering a total distance of 10,361 miles. It would be another year before the teams were ready to profit from their hard-won experience, and to try again to reach the all-important jet streams, and it was clear they would be joined by a growing band of hopeful rivals.

Back to the drawing board

At the end of 1997, Branson was ready to try again, but an accident while inflating the balloon saw it torn from their grasp by a sudden gust of wind. The envelope flew on its own into neighboring Algeria. To make things infinitely worse, Branson's engineer, Alex Ritchie, was fatally injured in a parachute jump during the wait for ideal conditions, and this put paid to another attempt. Meanwhile, Steve Fossett took off from St Louis on his second attempt, but once again bad weather at this lower altitude proved to be fatal to his hopes. Flying a more northerly track than before, he reached southern Russia before having to give up on his attempt.

Two of the new challengers were brought down soon after take-off by the same problem with their Rozière balloons. A solo contender, Kevin Uliassi, had taken off from Chicago, but two hours later the helium cell of his balloon burst, and he had to make a forced landing. Dick Rutan and Dave Melton took off from Albuquerque in New Mexico, only to meet the same problem, and escaped by parachute from the stricken balloon.

Most promising of the early 1998 crop of attempts was the second Breitling Orbiter balloon. This time Andy Elson, from the Himalayan ballooning expedition, had joined Piccard and Verstraeten. The balloon envelope had an outer skin of aluminized Mylar to reflect the sun's heat during the day, and minimize radiated heat losses during the night, with a polyurethane-coated nylon inner envelope containing the helium.

On top of the balloon was a smaller helium balloon which supported a cone of Mylar, with the interior of the cone cooled during the day by electric fans driven from solar panels. A lower hot-air cone, also of Mylar, was used to carry hot air from the burners up to the lower surfaces of the helium cell. The crew also needed to know the wind strength and direction at different altitudes, since the only way a free balloon can change direction is by ascending or descending to use a different wind direction. Masses of data were sent from a control center in Geneva, and from commercial airliners in the area of the balloon's flight.

ABOVE: *Switzerland's Breitling Orbiter 2 had an ingenious pressurized capsule design, but problems over access to Chinese airspace brought its round-the-world attempt to an end in Burma*

The Breitling Orbiter 2 proved to be a stupendous improvement on its predecessor, but it too failed to make it around the globe. The flight began at the end of January, with the capsule being shaken by a drop from its crane when being hoisted into position, and once again there were leaks from the hatches. Again they drifted south over the Mediterranean, trying to pick up the high-altitude jet streams, and consuming precious time and fuel in doing so.

Nevertheless, they set a new endurance record of nine days and 18 hours and traveled across Europe and most of Asia, but were eventually brought down by a new and much more difficult problem than bad weather or equipment failure. The Chinese refused permission for the balloon to enter their airspace after months of negotiation, and threatened to bring it down if it overflew their borders without permission.

All the crew could do was select winds that would take them to the south of China, and away from the all-important jet streams on their preferred direct route. Mounting worldwide pressure eventually made the Chinese authorities change their minds, but by then too much time and distance had been lost. Fuel shortages meant it would have been too dangerous to attempt to win back the lost ground and then attempt the long Pacific crossing, so they finally came down to earth again just 75 miles from Rangoon in Burma.

Steve Fossett too tried again, and this time managed to fly all the way to the Coral Sea, to the north of Australia, and on the threshold of the Pacific proper, setting a new endurance record of 15,200 miles. But it was clear that the limitations of his relatively unsophisticated balloon would never allow him to reach the jet

streams that would carry him round the globe while his fuel and supplies lasted. So, for the 1998–99 season, it was announced that he would join Richard Branson's latest challenge, with all the advantages of a truly high-altitude balloon, massive reserves of fuel, electronic navigation aids, and with the added luxury of a three-man crew to share the tasks of flying over such enormous distances with all the associated difficulties.

In many ways, the Branson flight of December 1998 was the most promising of all. By skillfully choosing their winds, they managed to navigate to the north of Iraq, to avoid the US and British airstrikes being made against Saddam Hussein's weapons systems. But once again China proved the intractable problem. Branson had permission to fly across the country on a narrowly and precisely specified corridor, but it was clear that earlier diversions would make their transit deviate from the agreement.

The Chinese, for their part, seemed to miss two points about balloons. Few craft are more harmless than a long-distance racing balloon, trying to cross the country as quickly and directly as possible, and no other flying machine is less capable of following a prearranged track. Once again, precious time was lost trying to avoid this enormous country, and once again the Chinese relented, but too late. Branson's balloon set out across the Pacific, but the jet streams failed to give them the progress they so desperately needed. In the end the balloon was forced to ditch in the Pacific, and once again the elusive target remained untouched.

Yet the most remarkable fact about the whole program of global ballooning was the fact that this furious competition was taking place at all. More than two centuries after Charles and the Montgolfiers had shown the promise, and the limitations, of lighter-

ABOVE AND OPPOSITE: *The 1998–99 Virgin balloon lifts off from Morocco with Lindstrand, Fossett, and Branson aboard, heading for an eventual touchdown in the Pacific*

than-air flight, people were still spending huge sums of money and vast amounts of ingenuity trying to extend the performance and endurance of balloons still further.

Here were balloons crossing huge oceans and vast continents, at stupendous speeds and at heights that verged on the threshold of space—though almost everything about these record-seeking craft would have seemed as exotic and frightening to the early pioneers as an alien spacecraft might seem to us. But the basic principles on which these flights were made would have been instantly familiar to them, thanks to the long, epic, and unbroken story of lighter-than-air flight. And they would have had no difficulty at all in understanding the queue of would-be record breakers waiting in the wings, even as the last global flight ended in an ocean ditching. If anything is certain in the never-ending history of ballooning, it is that sooner or later this hurdle too will be overcome.

Comforts and instruments

Modern long-distance gondolas, like that made for the Breitling Orbiter 2, are usually made from composites reinforced with carbon fiber and Kevlar. This had hatches designed to be sufficiently airtight, to avoid the need to run compressors to maintain the air pressure inside the capsule during the flight. If air *did* leak out on the journey, cylinders of pressurized oxygen and nitrogen would allow cabin pressure to be topped up at regular intervals.

Electrical power required for communications and navigation aboard the gondola was provided by batteries, topped up by a set of solar panels hung below the gondola. To help understand how the balloon performed in different weather conditions and at different times of the day, 14 temperature transducers were mounted at different positions on the envelope, and read and recorded every 30 seconds by the onboard computer.

Andy Elson (pictured above), designer of the Breitling gondola, has also designed the gondola for the *Cable & Wireless* round the world balloon, which would be the next one to attempt the so far unattainable. Once again, he planned to use kerosene for fuel, carried in lighter, unpressurized containers, and capable of burning at temperatures down to -130°F.

The two-man crew would have to rely on dried foods that can be prepared with a kettle at 185°F, as any more elaborate cooking at higher temperatures would cause the inside of the gondola to steam up. Other food stocks included dried fruit, hard cheese, cookies, and candy bars, with large stocks of water. Two bunks and a toilet, and a wide range of clothing to cope with temperatures from freezing to the equivalent of a warm summer's day, helped to keep the crew as comfortable as possible on the flight.

Communications devices included a Global Positioning System (GPS) receiver, which will fixed the balloon's position to an accuracy of 100 meters at any moment, using a network of US military satellites. The crew also had a VHF radio and a satellite communications terminal to link them to air-traffic control systems, passing airplanes, and their own mission control HQ. Data on the balloon's position, track, and speed was relayed every 30 minutes, during the course of the flight.

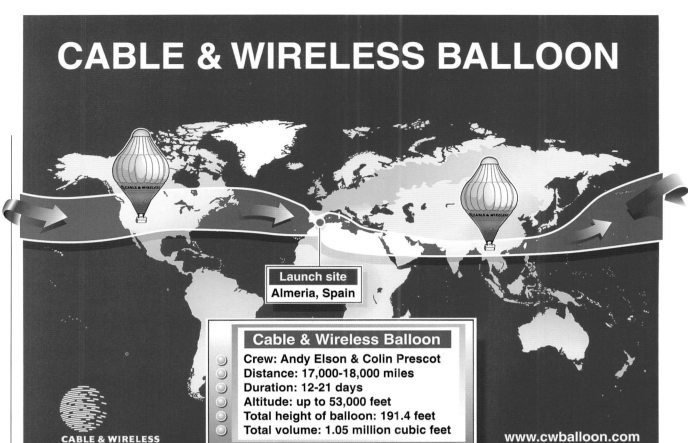

CABLE & WIRELESS BALLOON

The next contenders

Launch site
Almeria, Spain

Cable & Wireless Balloon
Crew: Andy Elson & Colin Prescot
Distance: 17,000-18,000 miles
Duration: 12-21 days
Altitude: up to 53,000 feet
Total height of balloon: 191.4 feet
Total volume: 1.05 million cubic feet

CABLE & WIRELESS

www.cwballoon.com

As the latest and most promising Branson balloon splashed down in the Pacific, the *Cable and Wireless* round-the-world balloon was waiting at its designated launch site at Almeria in Spain for the right combination of weather and wind conditions to start its record attempt. *Cable & Wireless* was another Rozière, but with a total capacity of 1.05 million cubic feet for extra lift and range. They intended to fly even higher than the other pressurized-gondola global balloons, where jet streams are faster and more predictable. Cruising altitude was 30,000 feet but the balloon was capable of reaching 53,000 feet.

The intended route was similar to that taken by the Branson balloon, over the Mediterranean and the Middle East, across India but rounding the southern edge of China before swinging northward across the Pacific, then across North America and the North Atlantic. For safety, the gondola was designed to float upright after ditching in the sea, and the crew carried parachutes, and

survival packs for all conditions.

Unfortunately, because of Branson's wandering from the authorized route over China, permission was denied for all British-registered balloons to enter Chinese airspace. Skirting the coast meant long delays, and they finally set out over the Pacific into increasingly stormy conditions. Finally they were forced to ditch off Japan, after setting a new endurance record, but the ultimate goal remained out of reach.

This left another six teams planning to mount round-the-world attempts as soon as conditions allowed. In Switzerland, the Breitling Orbiter 3 was using a modified gondola which reverts to propane burners after the experiments with kerosene. Two balloons were preparing in the USA. The *Spirit of Peace balloon* is being readied for launch at Albuquerque in New Mexico, while solo pilot Kevin Uliassi is to make a second attempt from Loves Park quarry, near his native Chicago, in a balloon named after his wife Renée.

Two more were hoping to avoid

political problems of the northern route by circling the globe in the southern hemisphere. The American World Quest team planned to launch from Santiago in Chile, while the *Global Conqueror* balloon was set to start from the west coast of South Africa. The joint Australian-American *Remax* balloon team planned to leave Alice Springs in Central Australia, to fly round the southern half of the globe in the opposite direction, across the Indian Ocean, South Africa, the South Atlantic, South America and the South Pacific.

Their helium balloon is designed to fly far higher than the others, at altitudes approaching 120,000 feet, leaving most weather systems far below. Americans Bob Martin and Dave Liniger and Australian John Wallington would have to wear space-suits for their planned 18-day flight, but problems with solar panels and excess weight led to the launch being postponed to the new Millenium, and the race was finally won by the Swiss-registered Breitling Orbiter 3 (see box on page 126).

Breitling Orbiter 3 makes round-the-world flight

The Breitling Orbiter 3, with Swiss pilot Bertrand Piccard and British pilot Brian Jones from the UK, finally lifted off from Chateau d'Oex in Switzerland on 1 March 1999. With the *Cable & Wireless* balloon leading them in the round-the-world race, they had a frustratingly leisurely start as their balloon drifted south and a trifle west across the Mediterranean and North Africa, searching for the vital jet streams. After two days they were still over Morocco, which had been the launching site for Branson's earlier attempts, but two more days put them into a faster airstream, heading towards Egypt.

While their rivals were coping with the problems of edging around Chinese airspace, the Breitling Orbiter encountered political problems of their own on the sixth day of the flight, with the southern Arabian republic of the Yemen denying permission to cross their airspace. Anxious maneuvers and a climb to 23,000 feet took the balloon clear of the prohibited area, and the following day the pilots were told of the ditching of the *Cable & Wireless* balloon, which left them the only contenders in the race.

On 8 March the balloon was crossing India, after a mixup over authorization which led to a ban on entering Indian airspace. Fortunately this was sorted out by the mission's control center in Geneva in time to allow Breitling Orbiter to follow a route to the north of Bombay, past Bhopal and into Bangladesh before approaching the all-important Chinese border.

By 10 March the balloon was safely past China, the first to meet the terms of their agreement to stay south of the 26th parallel. Overflying that vast country, thanks to favorable winds, took just 14 hours, leaving the crew facing the much wider hazard of the Pacific crossing. With problems of cold, dwindling fuel reserves and the lack of a favorable wind this was the most anxious time of the flight, but by 16 March the balloon was riding the jet stream at 100 knots towards the west coast of Mexico.

By 18 March the balloon was safely across Mexico and over the Caribbean with only the Atlantic ahead. Finally at 9.54 GMT on Saturday 20 March 1999, they finished their circumnavigation of the globe by crossing the latitude of their outbound track over the North African republic of Mauretania. Next day they reached Egypt again, in an attempt to enable Brian Jones to see the Pyramids which they had missed on their outbound voyage, but fuel shortages brought them down in the Western Desert, where they waited 8 hours for rescue.

Not only were they the first to travel non-stop round the world by balloon, but their overall time of 19 days had won them a $1 million prize. In using elements of the balloons of Montgolfier, Charles, and de Rozier, their achievement was one which those far-off pioneers would have understood, and appreciated.

Acknowledgements and Further Reading

Any book telling the story of a subject as complex and colorful as this one is a collaborative effort, based on information ranging from the anonymous artists and printers who immortalized the first flights of the pioneers to the writers and photographers of more recent times. For readers interested in exploring different facets of the subject in more detail, balloons and airships have produced a varied literature. Some of these books are long out of print but are still available from libraries, especially those with a special interest in aeronautical subjects.

For the earlier years of ballooning right through to the start of the twentieth century, *The Aeronauts* by L T C Rolt covers the achievements of the pioneers in detail, while Lennart Ege's *Balloons and Airships 1783-1973* takes the story from the very beginning right through to the first of the "new" hot-air balloons of the 1970s, with a wealth of colored drawings. *Man in the Clouds: The Story of Vincenzo Lunardi* by Leslie Gardiner, tells the story of Britain's first aeronaut; *Balloon Tytler* by Sir James Fergusson reviews the achievements of another pioneer, and *Ballooning* by C H Gibbs-Smith is a text book by one of the gas-balloon enthusiasts from the early twentieth century.

On more modern ballooning, *The Book of Balloons* by Erik Nørgard contains advice on taking to the air, which is echoed by the work of one of the pioneers of the hot-air balloon renaissance, Don Cameron's *The Ballooning Handbook*, published in 1980. Most recently, *Ballooning* by Anthony Smith and Mark Wagner covers most aspects of present-day hot-air balloons.

Literature on airships is equally varied, from Hugo Eckener's *My Zeppelins* to Joseph F Hood's *The Story of Airships: When Monsters Roamed the Skies. The Achievement of the Airship* by Guy Hartcup is a good general review of the subject, while *Airships: an Illustrated History* by Henry Beaubois and Carlo Demand has some unusual archive pictures from the early days of airship flight and a series of meticulously detailed color drawings. J Gordon Vaeth's *Graf Zeppelin* covers similar ground to *The Zeppelin Story* by W Robert Nitske and *Airships in Peace and War* by Robert Jackson. Finally Len Deighton's *Airshipwreck!* covers the sad fate of every major airship to be lost to weather, structural failure, or enemy action over almost a century.

Picture Credits

Royal Aeronautical Society page 8, 9, 10, 11, 12, 13, 14, 15, 16, 17, 18, 19, 20, 21, 22, 23, 24, 25, 26, 27, 28, 29, 30, 31, 32, 35, 36, 38, 40, 41, 42 (top), 43, 44 (bottom), 49, 51, 52, 53, 54, 55 (left), 56, 57, 58, 62, 63, 64, 65 (top left, bottom right and left), 68 (bottom), 70, 73, 74, 75, 76; ET Archive 37, 47, 48, 55 (right), 59, 67, 71; US National Archives 33, 34, 50, 77 (top left); Vintage Magazine Archive 39, 44 (top), 66; Daimler-Benz Archives 42 (bottom); Francois Prins 45, 46, 65 (top right), 69, 77 (top right); Henri Beaubois and Carlo Demand *Airships: an Illustrated History* 49; TRH Pictures 68 (top), 73 (bottom), 74 (top), 77 (bottom left and right); Peter Bish 1, 5, 72, 78 (top and bottom left), 86, 89 (bottom), 91 (bottom), 93, 95 (bottom), 96, 97, 98, 99, 106 (bottom), 110, 112, 113 (top left); Jerry Young 78 (right), 80, 82 (top), 83, 84 (left), 85, 87, 88 (bottom), 89 (top), 90 (bottom), 91 (top), 92, 95 (top), 100 (bottom), 101; Rekwin Archives 79, 82; Allsport 2, 3, 5, 84 (bottom), 88 (right), 124 (top left and bottom); Leo and Mandy Dickenson 88 (left), 90 (top), 114, 118, 119; Alex Larg 83, 94, 95 (right); Airship International Ltd. 102; Zeppelin Luftschifftechnik 103; Lightship Group 103 (bottom), 113; Cargolifter, Germany 104, 105; Airship Management Services 106, 107 (top); David Oliver 107 (bottom); Airspeed Airships 108; Institute of Design, Illinois Institute of Technology, Chicago, Illinois 109; 21st Century Airships 111; Lindstrand Balloons 117; Chaz Breton (Virgin ABC) 115, 120, 122, 123; Breitling 116, 121, 126; Cable and Wireless 124 (top right), 125

The Publisher would like to thank all the companies and individuals for contributing illustrative material and/or information in compiling this book.

While every effort has been made to trace copyright for all pictures used in the book and to ensure that all credits are listed, the Publisher apologizes for any omissions.

Index

Page numbers in *italic* type refer to picture captions